What if School Creates DYSlexia?

FHREE

FULL HUMAN RIGHTS-
EXPERIENCE EDUCATION

About the book

A must-read for parents and educators!

Some dyslexics never develop a reading problem, while others will struggle all their lives. What if School is what makes all the difference – but not in the way people think? Why do even our best attempts at remedial help too often backfire, causing anxiety, depression and damage to self-esteem?

If we can understand WHY only some dyslexics develop problems with learning to read while others do not, and what makes the difference, we may be able to change the lives of millions of young people. With adult dyslexics disproportionately represented among our most creative innovators and high achieving citizens on the one hand and the among prison inmates on the other, changing school-age realities could transform not only individual lives, but the well-being of our whole society. Given that between 5% and 20% of the population has dyslexia, how is it possible that young people in alternative education seldom if ever develop any problems around learning to read? Is there something - not only about the way that reading is taught, but about *when* it is taught and maybe also the fact that it is 'taught' at all - that makes it more likely that diverse learners will struggle? What if all of the common 'solutions' can actually become part of the problem, depending on whether they are offered, or imposed?

This book will leave you reeling with new possibilities, and concrete directions to explore.

About the author

Je'anna L Clements is an advocate for young people's rights, a writer, a mother of a teen and a tween who have both self-educated since birth, and a founding member of Riverstone Village, Africa's first Sudbury-inspired learning community. She writes articles and e-books on alternative education including Help! My Kid Hates School! and the Helping The Butterfly Hatch series of books on Self-Directed Education facilitation. Book One - How Does Self-Directed Education Work, and Why? and Book Two - How Can We Best Support Young People In SDE are available as e-books, and more volumes in the series as well as print versions are forthcoming.

What if School Creates DYSlexia?

By Je'anna L Clements

Copyright© 2020 by Je'anna L Clements
Published by FHREE in assosiation with ALLI asbl
www.fhree.org
www.alliasbl.lu
Cover Art by: André S Clements
Book Layout by: Max Sauber

ISBN: 978-0-620-91871-8 (paperback)
ISBN: 978-1-005-01144-4 (ebook)

Please Note:

1.   This book is not an academic or scientific research paper but a philosophical exploration demonstrating the urgent need for action supported by appropriate research.

2.   The scope of this exploration does not include alexia - reading problems acquired as a result of suffering brain damage.

3.   This fence-sitting text will variably refer to 'dyslexics' and to 'people with dyslexia'.

Dyslexia

Let us clip the wings of butterflies

so they will crawl as required

we have the wisdom to know

what matters, and should be

poor cripples,

we will heal you

of this crazy need to fly

sit down,

sit still

as we do

turn grey

Contents

The Start of My Own Journey

"There's never been a kid in our school – ever – who hasn't learned how to read, eventually, in their own good time. And we've never had a case of dyslexia in 47 years." - Daniel Greenberg, Sudbury Valley School

This particular quote is from a podcast interview that Daniel Greenberg did with Lenore Skenazy in 2014.[1] However, Greenberg has mentioned this fact in a number of his own writings. The first time I came across it (I don't recall whether it was in his book "Free At Last" or maybe "The Sudbury Valley School Experience"), I had to read it three times.

What?

Never?

It is commonly accepted that between 5% and 15%, maybe even 20% of people are dyslexic.

Sudbury Valley School has had many hundreds of young people pass through its doors over the decades. What's more, a disproportionate number of them arrived there after finding a lack of fit with other forms of education.

So, what is the statistical likelihood of not even one dyslexic student ever enrolling? How is that possible?

It seemed a big thing to claim, but by now I had read enough of Greenberg's work to trust his insight into the learning process, and he also struck me as someone with considerable personal integrity. In addition, when I searched the web, I couldn't find a single dispute of the claim, which surely would have surfaced by now.

And yet there it is, you can read it in the transcript for yourself:

"Lenore: You've never had a kid with dyslexia?

Dan: Not one."

---

1   At the time of writing SVS is now 53 years old and I have confirmed with Daniel Greenberg that nothing has changed there regarding dyslexia https://sudburyvalley.org/essays/conversation-about-svs

What is Dyslexia, Actually?

The simpler definitions of dyslexia involve the idea of a disorder that interferes with the ability to read. In German it's called "wortblindheit" - 'word blindness'. These days we know that there's a lot more to it than that.

On the downside, dyslexia can be associated with a number of different kinds of difficulties that impact both reading and spelling. It's a way of perceiving, processing and storing information that can lead to trouble understanding the link between letters and letter-combinations and their sounds. For example, there can be scrambling and inversion of words and letters - this is the 'symptom' most people associate with dyslexia. There can be a tendency to apparently predict or guess rather than read what is on the page, skip or misread short words such as 'as' and 'to', and struggle with abstract words more than with nouns. Memory retention of sight words can be hard to maintain - even just from page to page. Reading can be exhausting, and even when it's apparently mastered, there can be deficits in comprehension for what has been read.

In short, dyslexia can make it almost impossible to teach a young dyslexic to read, and if reading is learned, dyslexia in a school setting can still make it almost impossible to process the quantities of text required to 'keep up' with a mainstream curriculum and testing schedule. Even when reading is mastered effectively, dyslexics can still struggle with spelling - being able to read a word reliably and repeatedly does not translate to being able to recall the accepted spelling of the word at will. There can also be impacts on the kinds of rote learning, memory and concentration that current school systems rely on.

It used to be believed that the downside was all that there was - hence the label DYS-lexia, given that the Greek 'dys' is translatable as 'bad', 'difficulty', 'diseased', 'abnormal', and 'faulty'. Lexia is 'word' or 'language'.

People used to (and some still do) comment in surprise when dyslexics achieved significant career success 'in spite of' their dyslexia.

In the last few decades, we have increasingly come to realise that it is not in spite of dyslexia that people like Richard Branson, Steven Spielberg, Cher, Walt Disney and Albert Einstein succeed. It is actually because of their dyslexia.

Dyslexia has a very significant upside.

Dyslexic brains can sometimes struggle with the two dimensions of symbolic and standardised text precisely because they specialise in advanced abilities such as multi-dimensional processing, making connections, and creative image-ination. Some careers such as acting and film-making, engineering, music and art are particularly suited to the dyslexic talent. Many dyslexics excel at sports, entrepreneurship or various kinds of innovation.

Imagine someone driving a sports car in top gear while leaning out of the window holding dog leashes, as a way to walk the mutts. The car would stall. You might assume that it's broken, when in fact it's just being forced to go slower than it can comfortably manage in that mode.

Dyslexic brains come with high power modes that need to be set aside to some extent when engaging with flat, abstract text. As the young person featured later in this text said in Case Story 2, when he reads he has to 'change gears'.

Having these extra 'gears' is no disability. Quite the opposite. As dyslexic super-chef Jamie Oliver points out, the response to finding out that a young person is dyslexic, should be to congratulate them on their excellent luck! This is why you will find dyslexia advocates such as Oliver and Branson leveraging their celebrity status in support of the MadeByDyslexia movement, in an effort to change public perceptions.

What having 'extra gears' does mean, is that dyslexics do their best when able to live their lives their own way rather than trying to do what works best for other people. (Which you would think is a pretty obvious statement that is true for everyone, dyslexic or not. In fact I do think it's true for everyone. However, education departments of the world apparently disagree.)

We also now know that dyslexic brains don't always experience a reading problem.

According to the self-survey at www.madebydyslexia.org, I, the author of this text, am 'probably dyslexic'. Dyslexia often runs in families, and my father's response to reading the draft version of this book was a realisation that he is an undiagnosed dyslexic with dyscalculia. However, I was reading before I ever got to school (more on this, later.) My spelling is excellent, I left school carrying the English prize for my year and was placed in the top 100 students in my year for English in a national 'olympiad'. I was nonetheless considered an 'underachiever' for my IQ, have execrable handwriting, and have never managed to keep a room neat no matter how hard I try. I also struggled with the 'procedural' type of math/s taught in schools, barely scraping a pass thanks to lots of hard work and extra tutoring, only to find, at university level, that I was actually in the very highest percentile for mathematical ability, coming top of my class in both logic and statistics. I'm not going to write an e-book called 'What If School Creates Dyscalculia' - I will rather refer you to John Lockhart for "A Mathematician's Lament".

Estimates for the prevalence of dyslexia vary widely, but whether the truth is closer to 5% or to 20% either way it's still a huge proportion of humanity. If you think about it, these percentages mean that dyslexic brains are only slightly unusual, not actually 'abnormal' in any meaningful sense of the word. Dyslexia is a lot more common than having naturally red hair. Possibly even more common than having blue eyes. Maybe even more common than being left-handed (another 'problem' that exists largely thanks to schooled contexts.)

So, if I am conceding that dyslexia exists in its own right, what am I doing writing an book with a title that implies that it might be just a side effect of school?

Let's return to the opening of this book.

Sudbury Valley School (SVS) has not had a case of dyslexia, for more than fifty years. Statistically speaking they 'should' have had more than a hundred.

Given how many young people 'end up' at SVS after finding a lack of fit in mainstream schooling, SVS should have had a LOT more than a hundred!

But, they have never had a case of dyslexia. Not.

One.

We need to take a look at how this can possibly be, and what schooling might have to do with it.

One of the most widely accepted models of dyslexia, is the three part model developed by Uta Frith. This describes how at the biological level there is often a genetic origin, which at a cognitive level can result in specific processing deficits, and these can lead, at the behavioural level, to performing poorly in reading and writing. For me the key point is that Frith underlines the fact that there is "a vast gap between brain and behaviour, and that external influences will enter into the clinical picture."[2]

What if the answer to how SVS can have been permanently free of dyslexia for over 50 years, lies in an exploration of these 'external influences'?

To make it easier to explore our current mystery, given that not all dyslexics experience problems with learning to read (such as, possibly myself) perhaps it will be useful for the purposes of this text, to distinguish between

- Dyslexia - a form of dyslexic neurology that is mostly advantageous and

- DYSlexia - 'cases' of dyslexia that involve significant reading or other problems.

Sudbury Valley School must have encountered Dyslexia! Why didn't they - ever - encounter DYSlexia?

---

2   Paradoxes in the definition of dyslexia, December 1999 Dyslexia 5(4) DOI: 10.1002/(SICI)1099-0909(199912)5:43.0.CO;2-N

Why Does it Matter? The Short-Term and Life-Long Consequences of DYSlexia

Let's look at two people born within months of each other - let's take myself vs art-world legend and film man Sir Steven McQueen. Maybe I was born with a Dyslexic brain and he was born with a DYSlexic brain and that's all there is to that. In fact, maybe his DYSlexic brain is why he's a Sir and a legend, and I am not!

OR

Maybe I never developed DYSlexia while Sir Steve did, due to other factors in our lives. McQueen had to wear an eyepatch for a 'lazy eye'. I did not. McQueen had to cope with systemic racism at school. So did I, but I was 'white'. And there are obviously other factors, too - who knows which or what may have made a difference, both to our relative dyslexia and to our relative legendariness.

If the difference between Dyslexia and DYSlexia is merely a matter of genes and luck, then there's not much we can do about it. However, if it comes down to factors that we can change, then that's enormously important.

Because.

There's a huge range of possible outcomes for DYSlexia. Not everyone ends up a Sir. Lesser known than Sir Steve but at least as awesome is the founder of www.noticeability.org, Dean Bragonier. DYSlexic himself, and dad to a young person with the same neurodivergence, Dean believes that shame and self-esteem issues are absolutely critical for DYSlexics.

He makes the public aware of the disturbing fact that while dyslexics account for

- 35% of entrepreneurs,
- 50% of all the 'rocket scientists' at NASA, and a staggering

- 40% of all self-made millionaires...

they also comprise

- 35% of school dropouts,
- 50% of the adolescents in drug and alcohol rehab, and
- 60%-70% of those variously labelled as 'juvenile delinquents'.

Young DYSlexics have extremely high rates of depression and anxiety.[3]

A study of prisoners in Texas found that around 80% of inmates were functionally illiterate and almost 50% could be clearly diagnosed as DYSlexic.[4]

Last but by far the least, Neil Alexander-Passe and others have confirmed that DYSlexics are at significantly higher risk for self-harm and suicide.[5]

Bragonier points out that during the teen years, young people go seeking their 'tribe', and group identity is key to self-esteem. If a young DYSlexic isn't lucky enough to find a positive peer group based on common interests such as sport or music, the 'obvious' group for youngsters with low self-esteem is the people smoking behind the sheds and getting into shoplifting. It can be a downward spiral from there.

That spiral can go a long, long way down.

Let's leave behind Sir Steve and go somewhere very else.

When I was a teenager in South Africa, few criminals were more notorious than the infamous 'screw-driver rapist' William Van Der Merwe. After a premature release from prison in 1989 he added murder to his repertoire. His final victim managed to kill him in self-defence, by shooting him with his own gun in a complicated and very

---

3   https://codereadnetwork.org/wp-content/uploads/2019/03/Factsheet_ Dyslexia_and_Mental_Heal th.pdf
4   Prevalence of dyslexia among Texas prison inmates K C Moody 1 , C E Holzer 3rd, M J Roman, K A Paulsen, D H Freeman, M Haynes, T N James
5   Dyslexia: Investigating Self-Harm and Suicidal Thoughts/Attempts as a Coping Strategy https://www.longdom.org/open-access/dyslexia-investigating-selfharm-and-suicidal-thoughtsatte mpts-as-acoping-strategy-2161-0487-1000224. pdf

lucky maneuver while lying down with her hands handcuffed behind her back. Both his motives and his past were picked over in detail. He had claimed that he was motivated by the addictive feeling of power he had over his victims, that helped give vent to his feelings of disempowerment and rage against society. There were many other negative factors in his history, so maybe his DYSlexia is not significant. However, the court considered it absolutely key to his problems when he first appeared in front of them for attempted rape at the age of 19. They gave him parole on condition that he get remedial help for DYSlexia, in order to improve his self-esteem - perhaps it might have helped, but we will never know. He was in jail for multiple rapes before the year was out. Here's a poignant quote his mother reported from his childhood. "I can't read the words...The teacher just ignores me. The other children laugh at me. I'm not interested. I don't want to go to school."[6]

On the one side we have Sir Richard, Sir Steve, Sir Jamie, Dame Keira Knightly, Caitlin Jenner, Whoopi Goldberg and many magnificent more.

On the other we have William Van Der Merwe, and around half or more of your local prison population.

Maybe the latter were all born with innately criminal forms of DYSlexia, while the former were all born with some kind of more 'positive' DYSlexia? Sir Steve's movies go to some dark places, but he tends to react to injustice with feelings of hurt rather than rage.[7]

Enter Ameer Baraka - bringing us proof that criminal DYSlexics can turn their lives around - even to the point of switching between these two groups.[8]

Ameer actively attributes his life of crime to his experiences with DYSlexia. "I sit up there for about 10 minutes just floundering through a book not knowing any of the words. And I knew that day I was going to be a dope dealer," said Baraka of his school experience.

Off to a solid start as a convicted felon, he had an awakening while serving four years in prison. "Dyslexia mentally incarcerated me.

6   https://www.scribd.com/document/124571047/South-Africa-s-Famous-Crimes-1903-1987
7   https://www.theguardian.com/film/2014/jan/04/steve-mcqueen-my-painful-childhood-shame
8   http://kingbaraka.com/

Living in that mental prison without a release date was horrifying. Getting myself to believe that I can learn to read was a challenge I had to win." So learn to read, he did. He read Malcolm X. He read about Mandela. He created a more positive identity for himself. He got involved in acting. He got released from prison, but more importantly, he released himself from DYSlexia into Dyslexia. These days he's an author, actor, and dyslexia activist, as well as one of those self-made multi-millionaires.

These vastly different possible outcomes for DYSlexia make it morally imperative that we take action.

Of course a significant number of DYSlexics don't fall into either extreme. They're not criminals but also not celebrities, applying their brilliance in less ostentatious professions such as paleontology, physics, medicine, law, teaching, business, and more. (We wouldn't know about Erin Brokovitch if her story had not been made into a movie.) Even among these there are far too many living with unnecessary shame and anxiety, hiding their struggles from employers, and even from friends.

Aside from the extreme and brutal injustice of abandoning millions of people to an unfair fate, rooted in our failure to sufficiently support their right to education, there's an even bigger picture than that.

The human race is facing possible extinction. Even our best-case scenarios involve mass-scale suffering on an ongoing basis. We have many, many problems to solve. Dyslexics are a large proportion of our innovators not only in the arts but in the sciences, and in social entrepreneurship.

Since turning his life around, Ameer Baraka has not merely stopped being a problem for his local precinct. He has positively impacted the lives of countless, countless domino-ripple-effect others by mentoring youth, their parents and educators, and working to improve police-community relations.

As Dean Bragonier points out "There are a lot of problems facing today's society... some of the most creative, innovative minds are at this moment atrophying behind bars."

If it's possible to change that - surely it's worth pulling out ALL the stops?

9

What Are The Currently Popular 'Solutions', And How Much Can They Help?

There has been a growing boom in the number of organisations formed to help change dyslexic reality. One list I found named 32 of them but didn't include many that I know of. It's simply not viable to survey them all, but their work seems to fall into three main categories:

1. Public education and advocacy to inform more people about dyslexia and change public perceptions as well as dyslexic self-perception.

2. Training for parents, educators and therapeutic workers.

3. Support and resources for dyslexics in various forms - multisensory teaching and various kinds of remedial sessions, assistive tech, policies that allow for accommodations and modifications, etc.

MadeByDyslexia is one of the organisations doing really amazing work in this field, and their own website divides their work into: Changing Perceptions, Creating Solutions, and Getting Involved. If you are a parent or educator it's worth noting that in addition to their publicity program leveraging the social capital of multiple DYSlexic celebrities, they offer a dyslexic-positive self-assessment tool as well as many other free online resources. They promote early identification of dyslexia and structured phonics-based multisensory reading instruction, as well as offering tech resources in partnership with Microsoft, and advocating for accommodations and modifications to support young dyslexics in being able to cope better within the school system.

Let's concede for argument's sake that all of these things can indeed help a lot with DYSlexia. If so, how realistic are they to provide at scale, and how reliable are they?

Unfortunately, preventive measures and remedial assistance are not always effective. It turns out that supporting DYSlexics is actually a very complex and specialised task, and many young people receive insufficient help, or 'help' that doesn't help.[9] Even when reading problems themselves are resolved, the process itself often causes significant shame, anxiety and impacts on self-esteem.

Far from being the magic bullet that many of us wish it was, the famed Orton Gillingham method

a. Can require multiple hours of specialist one-on-one time that simply isn't feasible for everyone and

b. still has a "gap that persists between professional advocacy for O-G and the need for scientifically based and peer-reviewed research" supporting the efficacy of the method.[10]

Furthermore, Cathryn Knight set out to study teachers' understanding of dyslexia in England and Wales - locations that are relatively well resourced and have solidly established education systems. She found that many teachers did not have a solid understanding of dyslexia, nor solid confidence in assisting dyslexics. She concluded that "evidence-based teacher training, which informs teachers of the up-to-date research on the biological, cognitive, and behavioural aspects of dyslexia, is **essential** to combat misconceptions and ensure that teachers have more nuanced and informed understandings of dyslexia."[11] (Emphasis mine.) How reliably can education departments around the world actually achieve this?

It's such a worthy and noble aim to train every teacher, and support every parent. To identify every dyslexic before they even become DYSlexic. To develop foolproof support systems and guaranteed tools. To provide each and every dyslexic with all the resources necessary to minimise the negative impact of their DYSlexia as it unfolds. However, there are three fundamental problems with all of this.

1. How realistic is it to reach each and everyone one of these young people with sufficient and effective support and resources? Even in the most affluent schools in first world countries it's currently

9   https://cdn.intechopen.com/pdfs/35808/InTechThe_contribution_of_ handwriting_and_spelling_remediatio n_to_overcoming_dyslexia.pdf
10   https://en.wikipedia.org/wiki/Orton-Gillingham
11   https://www.ncbi.nlm.nih.gov/pmc/articles/PMC6099274/

a very utopian aim that frequently fails. How could we ensure that what's offered actually works not just for some, but for all? And are the young people in poorer communities and developing countries to be left to just keep falling through the cracks completely? MadeByDyslexia and similar initiatives are noble and determined and persistent - but even with involvement from giants such as Microsoft, they remind me of the inspirational meme about starfish on the beach.[12]

2. How much help is enough? Obviously this answer will be different for every DYSlexic. Some young people come out of remedial processes and absolutely thrive. Others come out still functionally illiterate in spite of it all. Yet others come out able to read at last but with horrible self-esteem that is at least as crippling as illiteracy. How could we effectively assess whether a young person has actually achieved their highest personal potential, or even whether the psychological damage on the way is significant or not? Ameer and William both went into jail and both came out - what made the difference between them? Can we afford to wait till we know?

3. Prevention is better than cure. IF there is any chance that dyslexics can be supported such that DYSlexia just does NOT HAPPEN in the first place, surely that would be 100 times better (although a lot less lucrative) than letting it happen and simply trying to minimise the negative results? Generally this possibility is not even considered, it sounds naive and too good to be true. But is it ethical to dismiss it without thorough investigation?

To date, when people other than myself have tried to draw attention to the possibility that allowing young people to use autonomous methods to learn to read might help in preventing DYSlexia, they have been met with nothing more than skepticism and summary dismissal.[13]

This is completely understandable. Our kids are precious. It's unethical to use them like lab rats (although unfortunately the school system does, all the time). But when it's something out of the mainstream and beyond the cultural norm it can feel as if the risks are

---

12   https://eventsforchange.wordpress.com/2011/06/05/the-starfish-story-one-step-towards-changing-the-worl d/
13   http://www.dyslexics.org.uk/uk_home_ed.htm

just too high.

However, there's just too much behind this possibility, and the potential rewards are too high, to continue to dismiss this out of hand, without at least taking a really good open-minded look.

To those who feel that it IS fair enough to dismiss these possibilities without thorough investigation -

- Are you really, really sure that you want to go down in history as one of the individuals who actively prolonged misery for millions and prevented something wonderful from happening, just because you can't be bothered to investigate properly, but prefer to rely on your prejudices?

- Or can you enter into a true Dyslexic spirit, go on an adventure together, and see what we do or don't find, when we actually take a detailed look?

> **Nobody can yet say for absolute sure what is or is not True about Dyslexia vs DYSlexia. But nobody can say that it's not worth the bother to find out.**

The stakes are too high for anyone to dismiss anything out of hand.

The MadeByDyslexia Microsoft training course provides the understatement of the century when it tells us that "If individuals with dyslexia are not identified or provided the proper support, their self-esteem can suffer."[14]

Dr. Gershen Kaufman, a psychologist specialising in shame, tells us that struggling with DYSlexia frequently induces levels of shame equivalent to that experienced by survivors of incest.[15] Even with remedial help. Sometimes in part because of remedial help.

But aside from what verges on trivialisation, there is an important phrase missing from that Microsoft sentence. To express the full truth, it needs to say "If individuals with dyslexia **who are immersed in a mainstream schooling system** are not identified or provided the proper support, their self-esteem can suffer."

---

14   https://education.microsoft.com/en-us/course/4acb190d/overview (module 2.3)

15   https://core.ac.uk/download/pdf/215520677.pdf

Daniel Greenberg from Sudbury Valley School presents us with the astounding possibility that individuals with dyslexia who are not immersed in a mainstream schooling system might never develop DYSlexia - or the associated shame - in the first place.

What if we don't have to deal with DYSlexia at all? What if we can actually head things off from the start in such a way that - like Sudbury Valley School - we never encounter DYSlexia at all?

Whenever we get to a point where we have to deal with DYSlexia, we're gambling with unknown factors that will influence whether we end up with another Sir Millionaire, another quietly brilliant citizen, another self-redeeming Ameer, or another femicidal Screwdriver Rapist.

If it's even remotely possible that DYSlexia need never exist and we can find ways to have only Dyslexia, then that's something we need to take very, very seriously.

And.

If you're not ready for the thought that all DYSlexia may be preventable, how about this thought...

What if...

What if we can reliably and significantly reduce the number of instances of DYSlexia?

What if the smaller number who turn out to really, really need the help can actually get it, because the queue for specialist services is only as long as it absolutely has to be?

Next Aha's In My Own Journey - Successful Illiterate Men: SAY WHAT?

Encountering Daniel Greenberg's claim to have no cases of DYSlexia was the first time radical thoughts about DYSlexia blew my mind. The first, but not the last.

A few years later, I happened across Roger A Clark's study of "Successful Illiterate Men" and my mind was blown yet again. In multiple ways. Firstly, I had to pause to unpack that title.

Illiterate men. Who were nonetheless Successful.[16]

Clarke points out that adult illiteracy interventions tend to be based on two faulty assumptions: "first, that literacy is a necessary precondition for success in life and second, that illiterate people are lacking in self-confidence, are unable to maintain employment, are poor, and are caught in a cycle of deprivation and under education."

Wow! These are exactly the same false two assumptions made by mainstream education systems. These two cultural myths are widely and deeply believed by parents, teachers - everyone. Until that moment, I believed them too! They are universally fed to young people as if they were fact, and to a young person busy developing DYSlexia, (and their parents) this message is terrifying.

And, it's false.

Wow. Just wow. It was already true in 1993 that you don't need to be able to read to make a success of your life. Sure it helped. But it was not a terminal issue! And now, in the next century when we even have text-to-voice and voice-to-text? The myth is even more hollow.

But that's not even the major mind blow I experienced from this study.

The second mindblow for me was the fact that Clarke uncovered

---

16   https://open.library.ubc.ca/cIRcle/collections/ubctheses/831/items/1.0055920

the fact that these men did not experience themselves as disabled by their lack of literacy, but they did find themselves disabled by the social stigma attached to their illiteracy, to the point that they generally had to hide the fact that they couldn't read, in order to succeed.

In other words, we, you and me, right now are actively creating a crippling disability for other people out of nothing other than our own prejudice and ignorance.This is huge. But it still wasn't the biggest mind-blow for me.

The biggest mind-blow was about the reasons the study was commissioned. The study was commissioned because the people providing adult literacy classes couldn't figure out why their offerings were not appreciated. Here they were, doing the saintly task of providing 'help' for these 'poor' guys, and these guys were walking out and not coming back.

Clarke nailed the reason alright. It became clear that men who have made a success of their lives don't appreciate being treated like charity cases. They were interested in learning to read, sure, why not. But classes that viewed them as disabled felt - at best - insulting. At worst such classes could trigger people back into the trauma of the disabling shame they've worked so hard to escape.

Clarke advised program designers that "a 'deficiency' oriented intervention program that over-emphasizes the importance of literacy diminishes the observable accomplishments of the illiterate adult and may fail." By 'fail' Clark means that the participants begin to feel shamed to the point that they just plain don't come back to class for another dose of shame. The only difference for young people in mainstream education is that they have no choice about coming back to class.

We are so used to treating young people as dependent and inferior that we find it hard to understand that young DYSlexics have the same kinds of feelings as adult DYSlexics.

As we will see in the next section, any intervention that focuses on inCompetence is bound to fail. So is any intervention that undermines feelings of Autonomy.

Aside from questions around how well conventional interventions for young DYSlexics 'work', there's a more fundamental problem. The bottom line for all of the current proposed solutions is that they all rely on the quality, training, and intentions of the people **around** the dyslexic, on the extent of accommodations allowed **to** the dyslexic, and on the quality of materials and tech provided **for** the dyslexic.

They leave dyslexics at the mercy of their socio-economic circumstances and other people's capacity and good will. Not only does this mean that dyslexics in poorly resourced environments will continue to fall through the cracks, it also means that dyslexics remain dependent, reliant on 'charity'.

All of these 'solutions' are well-meaning but paternalistic. They fail to empower and leverage the talents of the actual dyslexic person's self - such as self-sufficiency, creativity, and inventiveness. Instead they are based on a view of the DYSlexic as being unable to cope without outside help - which fundamentally undermines feelings of Competence.

Does keeping DYSlexics dependent and reliant on charity bolster self-esteem? Or induce shame?

Ummm...

Back to Frith's "vast gap between brain and behaviour" caused by "external influences" that "enter into the clinical picture."[17]

The final Aha's that led to my current thoughts about DYSlexia, came gradually, as I studied human motivation and well-being and their relationship to learning.

What if, instead of

'external influences' such as what age dyslexia is diagnosed or how it is remediated, it is actually the

'external influences' that mediate motivation and well-being,

that are the key influences that 'enter into the picture' to bring about the difference between Dyslexia and DYSlexia?

Let me unpack that a bit, and let's see what you think.

---

17   Paradoxes in the definition of dyslexia, December 1999 Dyslexia 5(4) DOI: 10.1002/(SICI)1099-0909(199912)5:43.0.CO;2-N

Understanding The Aha - Dyslexia, Motivation and Shame

Bear with me. I need to touch on some very involved concepts in a very brief way here. Maybe I can pull that off. If not, there's some suggestions in the 'further exploration' section to fill out the gaps I might leave.

Here's the pieces of the puzzle that I came across, and the way that my 'probably dyslexic' brain watched them slide into place.

1. From learning about behavioural neuroscientist Stephen Porges[18], I learned that:

We need to feel safe in order to learn well.

We don't have much ability to choose how to direct our attention when we're trying to survive - danger directs our attention for us. Different neurochemicals kick in depending on how safe or unsafe we feel. Even subtle levels of fight/flight/freeze states that are triggered by relationships or situations that feel unsafe, can interfere with learning.

When we are anxious our ears even adjust to help us pick up extremely high and low pitched sounds that might signal danger - growls and rumbles, fire-crackling and distant screams. Only when we relax do our ears tune in well to the normal ranges of the human speaking voice.

In other words, a person who feels anxious or fears being shamed, can't easily concentrate. Depending on their unique circumstances their bodies will tell them either to fight, to flee, or to shut down. In the classroom this can look like clowning around, acting up, getting distracted, or daydreaming. Chronically it can look like psychosomatic illnesses, school refusal, anxiety, defiance, 'zoning out', or depression.

---

18   https://www.stephenporges.com/

2. From learning about the Self-Determination Theory (SDT) of Deci and Ryan[19] I discovered that:

a. We all need three basic needs to be met, in order to feel safe and harness our motivation.

These three needs are absolutely universal for all humans (yes they checked this, thoroughly). They are:

Autonomy
making my own choices, being in charge of my own life, and doing things in a way that is meaningful and suited to my uniqueness.
Competence
feeling like I am good enough, I am capable, I can manage what I need to.
Relatedness
belonging, being valued, feeling connected and able to care and be cared for.

To the extent that these needs are met, I will be able to accept your support, respect your advice, and feel motivated to make use of what you offer me. To the extent that these needs are not met, I will struggle to trust you and will not feel motivated and will find it hard to comply with advice or support you try to give me.

Also from Deci and Ryan I learned that:

b. Autonomous Motivation is sustainable, Controlled Motivation is not.

What this means is that:

If it's my own idea and I want to do it for my own completely internal reasons, I will be able to stick with it and do whatever it takes and maintain my gains.

19   https://selfdeterminationtheory.org

> If it's your idea and you are persuading/encouraging/rewarding/threatening me, and I want to do it to please you/obey you/get the reward/avoid the pain then I will find it very hard to stick with it and will only be able to stay on task while you actively keep me at it, and will be unlikely to maintain my gains.

3. Last but not least, I learned by reading about Csikszentmihalyi's work on Flow[20]:

   We need an optimal balance between skill-level and challenge-level

   > If a challenge feels too much bigger than our current skill level can rise to, we become anxious, and disengage from the task.

   > If our skill level is too high for the challenge we face, we become bored.

When there's a challenge size just right for our next skills-stretch, we become so engaged we find it hard to stop engaging and learning. We're in the sweet spot. We excel. We learn. We grow. Humans enjoy learning more than almost anything else. This is why we master things for no other reason than the love of doing so.

We crave 'flow' states, they're key to our happiness and wellbeing. If certain activities fail to give us flow states, we will opt for those that do give us flow states. If our general anxiety levels are high, we will choose things that offer low levels of challenge. Only as we move into feeling safe are we able to engage with things that offer higher levels of challenge.

Last but not least, when it comes to pressure - once we are confident and highly skilled at something, a bit of pressure can help us hit peak performance. However, while we are still struggling to master a skill, pressure can kill off performance completely. This can lead to feelings of incompetence and shame, and make it almost impossible to improve our skills.

And so we come full circle to what I learned from reading Porges.

---

20 https://www.researchgate.net/publication/224927532_Flow_The_Psychology_of_Optimal_Experience

To sum up: try to get somebody else to do something you believe is good for them, in ways you think are right for them, while you stay in charge of the activity, and you generally

| undermine the relationship making it harder for them to receive your offering |
| making it harder for them to stay motivated and engaged, |
| making it more likely they will get poor results, |
| making it more likely they will feel shamed, |
| making it more likely they will become anxious, |
| making it harder for them to engage with the task as well as further undermining the relationship.... |

On the other hand: allow somebody to do what feels meaningful to them, in their own time and their own way, using you as an assistant as they wish, and you generally

| Increase their sense of safety as well as relatedness, |
| making it easier for them to stay motivated and engaged, |
| making it more likely they will get good results, |
| making it more likely they will feel Competent, |
| making it more likely they will experience Flow, |
| making it more likely that they will not only learn effectively but keep on loving the learning and doing more and more of it... |

What this adds up to is that teaching reading without consent is automatically going to make it harder for any young person to learn than if they have a genuine choice in the matter.

Add to that, teaching them in a way that doesn't fit their learning styles and you make it harder still.

Add to that doing it before their brain is ready and you make it harder still.

Add to that an environment where they feel pressured and even shamed, and where relationships are shaky, and you can make it almost impossible.

Add to that a dyslexic brain...

On the other hand... There is no critical period for learning to read. At the point that someone becomes Autonomously motivated, whether that's at 4, 7, 11 or 14 or even as an adult - like Ameer - that's when they're most likely to succeed.

If There Isn't Any DYSlexia in SDE, What IS there in SDE?

"We've never taught reading." says Daniel Greenberg, from the Sudbury Valley School, in the same interview with Lenore Skenazy.

If they don't teach reading at SVS, how do the kids learn it?

Sudbury Valley School practices a form of education that has variably come to be termed Self-Directed Education (SDE) and/or Natural Learning.

Bearing in mind what we've just looked at in terms of Motivation, here are two contrasting lists, probably not comprehensive, but covering a number of aspects of the learn-to-read process in SDE compared to the process in most types of school.

These lists are not in a particular order, but have rather been numbered so that you can easily contrast them point-by-point.

In Self-Directed Education (SDE) such as that practiced at Sudbury Valley School, young people learn to read

1. When they are ready, whatever age that may be. Usually this is somewhere between 4 and 14, with a rough average around 8.5 years of age. Before 4 and after 14 are also considered to be just fine, although they are extremely rare.

2. Sometimes in a short-term fugue of non-stop progress, sometimes in many installments over many years with lengthy periods of no apparent literacy activity.

3. Only when they choose to.

4. Knowing that they are valued, cared for, appreciated and allowed to stay whether or not they ever learn to read.

5. In synch with their own flow, fitting comfortably within their other activities and priorities.

6. According to their own biorhythms (you may notice that in both of the longer case stories below, all reading progress happened last thing at night.)

7. With no pressure at all - reading is no more or less rewarded than tree-climbing skills.

8. By methods of their own choosing, often of their own invention, methods which change and evolve as needed.

9. In ways that allow for a full expression of personal creativity, adventure and delight.

10. Within a supportive context where reading is not artificially elevated in importance, and where their progress is not judged or even evaluated.

11. Without shame - no staff member makes them feel that they should be able to read already.

12. In a way that supports them in feeling their progress and competence at every stage, rather than making them aware of the deficits still to be overcome.

How is this different to school? In school, children are taught reading:

1. At the age prescribed by the system, which may be as young as 4 in Montessori, usually 5 or 6 in public education, or as old as 9 in the Waldorf system. In other words, later than some children are ready and long before others are ready. Reading in the toddler years is considered to be 'hyperlexia' and most children unable to read by the expected age are considered to have 'learning difficulties'.

2. In measured installments that stay steady and consistent, continuously day after day without significant breaks, for years.

3. Without regard for their desires and often actively against their will.

4. Feeling that much of their value as people and positive feedback from others is conditional on their success and knowing that they can and will be separated from peers and adult helpers depending on their reading results.

5. Against their flow, in installment sizes prescribed by the system and without regard for their other priorities and activities.

6. Against their biorhythms at the times of day that suit the system.

7. Loaded with pressure - they are given both implicit and explicit messages that almost nothing matters more than reading.

8. By imposed methods, determined by the institution according to pedagogical philosophy and/or current fads.

9. In ways that not only discourage but actually penalise and sometimes even punish creativity.

10. Within a judgemental value system that both links literacy to personal worth and constantly evaluates progress in a judgemental way.

11. In ways that shame - there is an insistence that young people must work to manage what they cannot manage.

12. In circumstances that are stacked to emphasize incompetence and de-emphasize strengths and particle progress.

In other words,

- **SDE optimises for Autonomy, Competence and Relatedness, while most other education systems undermine all three.**

- **SDE allows reading to happen through Autonomous Motivation, while most other education systems rely on Controlled Motivation.**

- **SDE optimises for Flow while most other education systems actively prevent experiences of Flow.**

What is the outcome of these two different types of approach to education?

For the non-SDE systems, the bulk of young people are reading at around age 6 or 7, with some - in America maybe as many as 19% - not achieving functional literacy at all by the time they leave school.

For SVS, it's zero functional illiteracy, and a wide span of ages at which young people have learned to read, without much difference in the final picture between those who learned 'early' and those who learned 'late'.

"What we have had is children who have started reading at a very wide range of ages. We've had some who started at four or five (that's what everybody likes to hear) and we've had others who started at nine, ten, even later. When you look at a person who isn't reading at the age of eight, you know that person in a standard school setting would be put in a remedial reading class and subjected to enormous pressures. But if you stay your course, as we have stayed our course over the years, and you leave that person alone and let them develop at their own pace, the "miracle" always seems to happen. By the time they leave, you wouldn't know the difference between those who started reading at four and those who started at eleven." - Daniel Greenberg, The Sudbury Valley School Experience.

Of course one of the enormous impacts of a failure to learn to read young, is the knock-on effect for the rest of the educational career - if you're in a mainstream schooling system.

Most schools push early reading in order to create a foundation for other learning, and young people learning as late as many at SVS would be severely compromised.

So, it's also important to look at the educational picture beyond just literacy. How do young people learn when we compare the two systems with regard to the rest of what we commonly consider to be 'education'?

In Self-Directed Education such as that practiced at Sudbury Valley School, young people learn skills and content entirely through self-chosen activity. Nobody else decides what you should or shouldn't do (within the bounds only of other people's rights, and the school rules.)

Most learning happens through direct life experience, open-ended experimentation and play. Conversation is probably the primary medium for giving and receiving information, and argument and debate are a common way to explore and integrate what is being learned. Active age mixing means that young people with more knowledge or experience consolidate their learning by assisting others who are still grappling with the basics, and in turn, the beginners get personalised assistance from learners who are just a few steps ahead and still able to relate to the struggles of a half-formed grasp of the material.

In SDE, observing other people in real life activity is often a way for learning to begin, followed by one's own experimentation and co-operative activity, often leading up to learning through direct relationships with mentors for advanced levels of skill.

It's also increasingly common to learn from watching videos. Obviously plenty of learning still happens though reading - but this is optional, depending on preference. Likewise many young people in SDE learn by writing and documenting - or not, again depending on preference.

Where learning happens as a result of engaging with challenges set by other people, this is completely optional and voluntary.

In other words, although reading is useful to young people in SDE, they are free to learn as much as they like in other ways. The world at large provides an incentive to learn to read, immersion in a literate environment makes it easy to the point of inevitability, but there's not an actual pressure to learn to read. And if - as has never happened yet - some young person did not learn to read, they would have intact confidence and many other well-developed coping skills to be at least as educated and capable as Clarke's Successful Illiterate Men.

How is this different to mainstream school? In school, children 'learn' primarily through reading, writing and documenting. If they can't do these three things, most of the other resources offered are closed to them. They also learn from listening to lectures, filling in worksheets, rote memorisation, completing mandatory assignments, and generally following instructions - even for work that is meant to be 'experiential'. They are age-segregated, the system is inherently competitive, and attempts at collaboration are disallowed as 'cheating'. None of this is conducive to meeting Motivational needs and very little of this provides opportunities for Flow states.

So: How Could School Create DYSlexia?

Given what we know about motivation, it's easy to see why young people can harness their full motivational drive to overcome all obstacles to reading when they are embedded in Self-Directed Education. It even makes sense of Ameer Baraka's sudden ability to learn to read in prison, when he hadn't ever managed until then.

On the other hand given that motivation and learning ability are impacted when we feel that other people are in charge of our actions, when we come to doubt our own competence, when relationships are damaged, and when we feel anxious - it's easy to see how even non-dyslexic young people often come to develop a level of 'reading allergy' when pushed to learn to read at school.

As Csikszentmihalyi points out "Many people stop learning after they leave school. The long years of education often leave behind unpleasant memories. Their attention manipulated by text books and teacher, they look at graduation as the first day of freedom."[21]

Contrast this 'norm' with the fact that SDE facilities often have to deal with young people loving 'school' so much they don't want holidays, their passionate enjoyment and delight in learning, and the unusually high proportion of SVS graduates who go on to tertiary studies...[22]

"Dysteachia" is a term for problems that result from inadequate instruction, and it's often used to point out that teachers need training in multi-sensory phonics-based reading tuition methods.

But What if Dysteachia is an even more telling word than that?

What if it is not as much the style of teaching, but the imposition of teaching that is the problem? What if any kind of teaching, no matter

21   https://www.academia.edu/41289200/Flow_The_Psychology_of_optimal_experience

22   Democratic Schooling: What Happens to Young People Who Have Charge of Their Own Education? Peter Gray and David Chanoff, American Journal of Education, Vol. 94, No. 2, The University of Chicago PressStable, http://www.jstor.org/stable/1084948

how competent, that is imposed against the deep consent of the learner, is at the heart of the problem? Not only for DYSlexia, but for all of the other forms of misery and failure we currently consider 'just part' of school?

A more detailed discussion of these dynamics is beyond the scope of this book but can be found in the first of my books on SDE facilitation: Helping The Butterfly Hatch, Book 1: How Self-Directed Education Works and Why (See Further Exploration section at the end of this text.)

So here's my hypothesis. It's perfect that Greenberg says "we've never had a **case** of dyslexia" (emphasis mine). It's not that they never had any dyslexics enrol. It's just that none of those dyslexics ever developed a 'case' of DYSlexia, precisely because nobody tried to 'teach them' to read.

In fact this is exactly what Greenberg says in The Sudbury Valley School Experience: "It could be an accident. The students who attended SVS might just happen not to be in that 10-15%. But it doesn't work that way. There's no pre-selection of non-dyslexic people in this place. We haven't had dyslexia because we haven't brought it about."

Let's play with possibilities just for fun. Let's return to myself and Sir Steve. Born in the same year, but I was born in August, and in a place where the school year starts in January. He was born in October, in a place where the school year starts in September. I'm betting he started school a month before turning six, while I started at six and a half.

We already know that in age-segregated and standardised educational systems 'summer born' children are often at a disadvantage due to their lack of physical maturity relative to their peers.[23] I learned to read in my own time and my own way - I don't know exactly when. Let's just pretend for a minute that it was when I was exactly six and four months, and that Sir Steve and I were soul twins, and that he would - left to his own devices - have done exactly the same.

Except that by then, other people had been trying to get him to read - in their way, under pressure - for a third of a year already. It is completely plausible that this could have interfered with his confidence and motivation sufficiently to make the difference between his

---

23   https://www.jstor.org/stable/1050142?seq=1

DYSlexia and my 'probable Dyslexia'. Had I been born in the Northern hemisphere I might have shared his fate.

Next, let's imagine a different soul twin - someone born ten years ago. My own pre-school experience was of the old-fashioned kind - sing-songs and nursery rhymes, finger painting, playing with other tots, listening to stories and getting muddy. My this-century twin more likely would have been given desk-work by the age of four. This also could make the difference between my 'probably Dyslexia' and their DYSlexia.

How Might Alternative Education Facilitate Dyslexia without Creating DYSlexia?

Next to enter our journey, is a literacy expert who specialises in teacher-training, who has spent multiple decades in Australia and America studying the classroom habits of teachers whose students achieve exceptionally high levels of success in learning to read.

It is interesting to me that although Brian Cambourne does not appear to be acquainted with Self-Directed Education, through studying success in literacy learning he has independently arrived at many conclusions that align with aspects of SDE.

For example, he emphasises the importance of the message that "It is safe to "have-a-go" in this setting."[24] He also emphasises that children should be given responsibility for their learning, be supported in constructing their own 'approximations' which should be affirmed rather than marked as 'mistakes', and trusted to learn in their own time, with as little hurry as possible.

This suggests to me that to the extent that any educational facility deeply respects young people as protagonists in their own learning as well as creates an environment of safety where there is little stress about literacy learning, they could facilitate Dyslexia more often than DYSlexia.

Sure enough, during the course of writing this book I discovered that Sudbury Valley School is not the only alternative school to encounter a complete lack of cases of DYSlexia.

Celestin Freinet, a French educator, founded not only one school but a whole "Modern School" movement back in the 1920's. After decades of experience, by the year before his death in the mid 1960's, Freinet had come to the conclusion that dyslexia simply did not show up in his form of education. Watching the gradual increase of dyslexia cases in other forms of schooling he speculated that it was a result of the

---

24   http://www.cambournesconditionsoflearning.com.au/

"growing difficulty for children to comply with school practices".[25]

Freinet found confirmation for this speculation in the work of French psychologist Roger Mucchielli, author of "Dyslexia, Malady of the Century", whose work led him to the conclusion that reading problems were a result of young people feeling pressured by the 'duty' to read. Freinet schools, by removing this 'duty' and allowing young people to take ownership of their learning in a more empowered, positive and less coerced way, did not produce cases of 'dyslexia'. He concluded that "except in rare cases of organic deficiency, dyslexia is a product of the school."[26]

When it comes to forms of Self-Directed Education practiced in ways and places other than school, Karl Wheatly goes so far as to actively suggest that schools could improve their literacy outcomes by taking inspiration from Unschooling, where also, young people are in charge of their own learning and under no pressure to read. He points out that "the approach to learning to read that is most effective in the long run in classrooms is interest-based learning that is connected to real life and that has large doses of freedom and choice. That is, while traditional reading instruction is actually one of the leading causes of reading problems."[27]

In answer to the thought that in all of these instances so far, the community of young people was possibly in various ways self-selecting and may have had exceptionally autodidactic temperaments, I came across the very interesting 30 year existence of the 'School of the 3rd Kind' facilitated by Bernard Collot.[28]

This was not an independent or private school, but a unique situation within a public school where the dissolution of several classes circumstantially led to Collot finding ways to deal with an age-mixed classroom for all primary school levels up to age 10. Faced with the unusual challenge presented by not being able to teach age-segregated grades, Collot drew inspiration from both Freinet and Montessori.

Gradually, in a process that sounds like the usual process that

25   https://www.icem-pedagogie-freinet.org/node/34825
26   Ibid
27   Wheatly, How Unschoolers Can Help To End Traditional Reading Instruction, Journal of Unschooling and Alternative Learning 2013Vol. 7Issue 13
28   http://freetolearnluxembourg.eu/Free_to_learn/EN_Bernard_Collot_files/ Bernard%20Collot%20Luxembou rg%2007.10.2017.pdf

'home-schooling' families often go through, progressively prioritising young people's well-being and best interests, to organically find that they have become Unschoolers, this section of the school became a place where young people had full educational autonomy.

Parents who held the 'fair enough' expectation that their children would cope well with the transition to regular high school work at age 11 were not only satisfied, but the model worked so well that the village chose to sustain it for as long as possible - which meant that eventually Collot had a full three decades of experience to draw on.

He remarks that statistically speaking, there must have been multiple dyslexics in his progression of classes, yet he never once encountered a case of DYSlexia. Here's what I managed to translate using Deepl free version: "I can tell you that all the children in my school have learned to read, to write at one time or another, each in their own way. Of course I helped them at those times to find their bearings, to understand and make themselves understandable, but I am unable to say whether it was through the elements I brought them that they learned. I'm even sure that their brains had used many other reference points drawn from the informal writing in which they were immersed in my school and elsewhere. Not one of them was learning in the same way. The important thing for me was no longer to make children learn what I had planned and paid for them to learn, but to give them all the conditions so that they could develop the tools to learn themselves." As for conventional methods of reading instruction, Collot cautions us that "Methods are very often inhibitory when we force the brain to work the way we think it works".

My (very quick, modest and informal) outreach to the alternative education community in the course of writing this current text, also yielded a response from alternative education veteran Jerry Mintz. Jerry recalls that the Modern School in the USA which was part of the movement initiated by Spanish anarchist Francisco Ferrer (a different 'Modern school' to Freinet's), which operated from 1914 to 1953, also didn't push students to learn to read - with no negative outcomes. Jerry recalls that one particular student from those times "wasn't interested in learning to read until he was 10. Then he wanted to read a particular book. His mother asked why he wanted that book when he couldn't read. He said, 'I'll learn to read that book!' Months later he was reading voraciously. He eventually got a scholarship to Columbia Medical school and became a famous pediatrician. I met another one there who didn't learn until he was 9 and became a psychiatrist."

My outreach also led to my receiving news about an alternative school in Canada, sadly now closed after almost fifty years of successful service, due to technical changes in district funding. The philosophy of the school was unique to its founder, but was essentially non-coercive and provided educational autonomy, while also actively offering - unlike Sudbury Valley School - a range of methods for literacy support. Rather than pursuing an either-or approach, the school embraced the idea of whole language within an immersive literacy environment, with a focus on high-interest words, but with phonics information shared with readers who were busy learning. Funny and engaging beginner books were provided rather than just boring 'readers'.

I am told that from 1971 till 2019, every single student learned to read eventually, and no student expressed regret at not having been 'made' to read earlier. Again - when the rest of education is not held back by being unable to read, there is plenty to explore and enjoy until reading readiness arrives. Also, when there is a culture that immerses young people in demonstrations or literacy but that nonetheless does not artificially prize eye-reading, there is little social discomfort for those who come to it 'later'.

The interesting thing about this more active provision of literacy support in the Canadian school, is that it was clearly visible that a very small number of students did not make significant progress in spite of their efforts and in spite of all the support offered. These young people showed other signs of DYSlexia such as later being unable to spell, and struggling to get their thoughts down on paper, and as suitable technology became available, being greatly relieved to be able to use it. However, what this school found was that, without exception, the picture changed after puberty.

Somewhere between the ages of 12 and 14 they all somehow managed to learn to read, all with excellent comprehension, reaching grade level within a year.

What if...

What if Greenberg, not paying any particular attention to anybody's learn-to-read process (because it's actively against SVS policy to

35

evaluate anyone's 'progress'), simply gave each and every student long enough for even the tiniest percentile of young people to transmute their own DYSlexia into Dyslexia?

That's quite a thought. The clincher for me is this: both Greenberg and Freinet actually did engage with young people who came to their schools illiterate and already having been - elsewhere - diagnosed with DYSlexia.

Here's a piece of evidence that comes to us via researcher Dr. Peter Gray. "In my study of Sudbury Valley graduates, two of the respondents told me, independently, that they had come to the school as teenagers unable to read. Both had been passed along from grade to grade, in public school, with a diagnosis of dyslexia. Both told me that they learned to read within a few months after enrolling at Sudbury Valley. When I asked why they could learn there what they had been unable to learn before, they both told me, in effect, that for the first time in their lives nobody cared if they could read. The pressure was off. Now, in a relaxed way, they could concentrate on reading. They didn't have to hide behind a label." Critically important to another question many people have around whether SDE simply masks significant problems, Gray adds that "Both went on to college, with no designation of dyslexia or any other learning disability, and performed well there." [29]

And I found this from Freinet (using free Deepl automatic translation software, sorry!)

"...there are no dyslexics in our classes. And this for children who start their learning according to our pedagogy.

"If they suffered, during the first years of this confrontation with "must-read" and "must-write", they risk being marked for all their schooling, as by the consequences of an illness.

"Healing is all the longer and more difficult the longer the child has suffered from this confrontation.

"It took us three years to re-educate a child who was massacred

29   Peter Gray's Chapter (3 :Children's Natural Ways of Educating Themselves Still Work: Even for the Three Rs) in Berch and Geary's book Evolutionary Perspectives on Child Development and Education.)

up to the age of 10 as much by the bad school methods as by the bad remediation that had been imposed on him. In this rehabilitation I noticed that the most serious consequence is that the child had totally lost the natural notion that one writes to say something and that what one reads must also mean something. Words no longer placed in their vital cultural context no longer had any specific figure: the child writes and reads them at random from his distorted school memories.

"Our dyslexic has made us a beautiful poem today, with still some mistakes, of course, but he is healed and saved."[30]

In other words, it looks to me like the message that learning to read is critically important, the expectation that young people 'must' keep working at it, and the pressure and potential shame that go along with all of this, as well as the strain it puts on young people's relationships with their adult companions, can actually prevent the development of competence at reading and cause stress-induced, life-long 'cases' of DYSlexia.

(What if... the huge range in the estimates of the prevalence of dyslexia, of between 5% and 20% could be due to the fact that actual dyslexia affects more like 5% while the other 15% are simply more sensitive to stress, strong-willed, or reliant on positive relationships and therefore less resilient in the face of mainstream school's assault on their autonomy, competence and relatedness?)

The key to deliberately 'healing' DYSlexia for Freinet seems to me to be centred in actively building a sense of positive Relatedness along with giving big doses of Autonomy along with positive relationship messages that lead to increases in perceived Competence.

The key to 'healing' DYSlexia at SVS as an unintentional but happy side effect of the deeply egalitarian treatment of young people, seems to me to be grounded in deep Autonomy, along with implicit support for unconditional assumptions of Competence, within a space of positive Relatedness.

---

30   https://www.icem-pedagogie-freinet.org/node/34825

"The Plural of Anecdote is Not Evidence"

This aphorism was coined by political scientist and lecturer Raymond Wolfinger. The funny thing is that public use has turned it on its head. Here is his protest. "I said 'The plural of anecdote IS data' some time in the 1969-70 academic year while teaching a graduate seminar at Stanford.

"The occasion was a student's dismissal of a simple factual statement—by another student or me—as a mere anecdote. The quotation was my rejoinder."[31] (Emphasis mine.)

Of course the plural of anecdote is data! That's exactly what qualitative research IS. And when it comes to the social sciences, to human reality and information about how we learn best, then quantitative data tends to lose the real information by reductionism. Let's note - it is the reduction of a student's achievements to quantitative data that 'proves' that a person with DYSlexia is stupid. It is only by taking seriously their qualitative anecdotal evidence, that we realise that they are not.

Just as quantitative data can be cherry picked and manipulated, so can qualitative data. It's always foolish to jump to conclusions - in either direction - based on minimal evidence.

I have not mentioned the multiple, multiple anecdotes from home education, nor even the formal studies of learning to read in home education[32] simply because it's already historically clear that there's standing cultural prejudice against home educators, and attempts to share their wisdom with the schooled world have already repeatedly failed - sadly for the young people who could have had happier lives.

What I am exploring right now is what has emerged from several completely unconnected schools in different countries, each of which had decades of experience behind what I share from them here.

---

31 http://blog.danwin.com/don-t-forget-the-plural-of-anecdote-is-data/
32 But there's a few links in the Further Exploration section, if you're interested!

If that's not the kind of evidence that convinces us that there's something to carefully consider, then what is?

Is There Any Place For DYSlexia Remediation in SDE?

As I prepared to write this book, I sent out a call to a number of facilities inspired by the Sudbury Valley School to find out what their experiences have been regarding dyslexia. I received very few responses - maybe due to pandemic conditions, maybe due to most SDE facilities just not being very interested in a subject that doesn't much affect them, or to having nothing to report because, like Greenberg, it's not something they've encountered. Given that there's no set age by which young people in SDE are 'supposed to' learn to read, it is very, very rare for a young person in SDE to need more help than any handy literate adult can give - such as telling them how to spell a particular word.

Generally SDE folks confirm that young people - including those diagnosed with DYSlexia elsewhere - who are given rich environments and plenty of access to supportive adults (and other optimising conditions for SDE that I won't go into here) can be trusted to figure things out for themselves, and ask for whatever help they need, once they decide they need it.

One response came from Melissa Graham, who used to work as a reading specialist in mainstream schooling before becoming convinced that it was worth the effort to cofound a 'Sudbury' type facility that she now runs. Aside from being a reading specialist, she's also a Dyslexia-mom whose son started reading at 11. I asked her if she thought there was ever a place for proactively intervening in a young person's reading process without being asked to do so. She replied "The only reason someone needs to intervene is to hijack the potential for the person to begin to tell themselves a negative self-story. The importance of naming a dyslexic a dyslexic is to protect their mental space and to guide/support the narrative into one that sings: Dyslexics are Brilliant! I was fortunate to discover that not one dyslexic is alike. They are all so very different and unique."

The need to prevent negative self-stories was confirmed in an ironic way by another mother who is staff at a different model of non-coercive alternative school. Her experience is that "reading and math can be stymied when forced prematurely and the skills can be learned at any age when the person willingly takes it on - there is no developmental window. It only takes a few months once people go for it, and reading the books they want to is the best way to gain fluency. But culturally, it's another matter. My kid's first book was Jurassic Park at age 10. He'd loved the movie and wanted the experience to last so he sat on his bed with that book for a month and grasped the skill of reading. A happy story. But I much later learned that he actually thought he was stupid for mastering it later than his peers, and he never really got over that. He thought everyone loved him too much to tell him! Talk about a backfire!"

What if...

What if his thought that he was stupid, possibly delayed his reading? What if, without that perception, he might have had the confidence to learn at 9? This issue is addressed in the final section of this book.

What's important to note is that the efforts of MadeByDyslexia to create public awareness around the upside of dyslexia could make a significant difference to experiences like these.

In the process of writing this book I was also fortunate to be able to chat with Justine McConville, a reading specialist who offers reading assistance to young Unschoolers who request it, while also being staff at the SDE Village Free School. She confirmed that she does see young people in SDE who are struggling, who do want help - although generally it is after they have already taken some damage in mainstream education, or from social influences that buy in to cultural myths and prejudices. The critical thing for her, is that young people must remain in charge of the relationship and the help that is offered. "I only aspire to be in consent-based relationships. I (have previously) had the experience of being with kids who were not there by consent and it's just wrong relationship, it burdens them emotionally even more, with the relationship they have with their own academic identity and then on top of that they have to do something against their will to fix what's 'wrong' with them." (My transcription of spoken words during a conversation I had with her.)

Both of these responses embed the idea of supporting Autonomy,

Competence and Relatedness.

I invite you to watch a powerful conversation between Justine and a mainstream remedial teacher Lynn, exploring the kinds of insights that I explore for myself with this text. If there's one and only one further thing you explore around DYSlexia, it should be this: Talking About Dyslexia: A Conversation Between Lynn Chambers and Justine McConville.[33]

When searching for potential criticisms of the perspective explored in this text, online, I have seen that some people worry that young people with dyslexia in SDE will simply go undetected, creating an impression that there is no problem, when in fact the problem is simply being left to get worse. Terminally worse. What they're missing is the fact that young people in SDE are empowered. They're not sitting stuck invisibly at the back of some classroom languishing for lack of attention. They're used to making progress and achieving what they choose to achieve, and get openly and obviously frustrated when they get 'stuck'. SDE kids are embedded in relationship. The few who do struggle with reading are very visible to the people around them, and they're free to ask for help. They may even be proactively offered help, especially if their frustrations make them cranky and disruptive to others. However, their decisions about whether, when and what help they do or don't need are respected. So far I have yet to find even one single story about a young person in SDE who had not thoroughly resolved their reading struggles by the age of eighteen.

It's not that young people in SDE are unable to get help if they genuinely need it. It's that it isn't imposed on them. It's that when it is done, it is with their deep consent - the kind of true consent that involves mutual desire rather than resigned acceptance, or capitulation out of fear when given the message that the other options will be even worse.

Illustrating this beautifully, I received a message from a mother who is also staff at a 'Sudbury' type school, with four children of her own. The eldest two learned to read easily without help, between the ages of 8 and 9. However the third child, whom we will call J, became increasingly stressed about reading after trying at 7, at 8, and still at 9. She was trying and trying and making no progress, and her mother could not work out whether the problem was motivational or something else. J was becoming increasingly frustrated, and demanding help

---

33   https://youtu.be/KKJMmnQZcMU

that her mother and others around her did not know how to give, so a reading specialist was sourced. J decided she would like to try a session - during which it became clear that she was struggling with DYSlexia.

Since 'Sudbury' schools bring in staff as needed and requested by young people, and J actively chose to have help with reading, the reading specialist came in to school for around an hour a week to help her for around 2 years, until at 11 years old she felt she no longer needed the sessions any more. Throughout the process, J was in charge of the relationship, choosing the day and time for sessions, free to end sessions early when she chose to, and also choosing what to work on, including help with learning her lines for the school play. Ms.S also introduced J to cursive writing, something that many dyslexics find easier than print, and J took to it with enthusiasm.

"It wasn't that Ms. S was teaching her, more like she helped J decode and it all clicked very easily for J. I think because it was truly coming from her. She is so happy and empowered that she was in control of her learning to read and write. It is so great to see the 2 things that frustrated her most she fully enjoys now. She loves art and manages her own instagram drawing page as well," says her mother.

In an interesting twist that's quite common in SDE to the surprise of people who haven't seen young people self-direct their screen time, J's reading also took a leap as a result of video gaming. "J had been reading the graphic novel of 'Wings of Fire". She didn't feel ready for the chapter books yet. Unfortunately while playing an online Wings of Fire game, in April 2020, someone let out some spoilers that are only in the chapter books. Well that propelled her to take on the challenge!"

This mother's youngest also has obvious Dyslexia, but chose not to have help from Ms.S. She successfully taught herself to read at the age of 10, without any specialist help.

Did Daniel Greenberg never encounter a situation like J's? Is J dealing with a case of super-severe ultra-rare level of DYSlexia that he would have encountered if his school were bigger? Maybe. My first thought was that maybe, it's just a matter of the level of struggle that's tolerable for a mother to watch. At Sudbury Valley School it's part of the philosophy that young people grapple deeply with things, struggle with things, and don't get 'rescued' unless they turn around and ask for what they need.[34] However, J read my first draft and corrected me. Her mother did not 'rescue' her. J's determination is very strong, and nothing was going to stop her learning to read right there and then no matter what. If she had been at Sudbury Valley School, she would likely have ensured that a reading specialist was engaged there too, as there was absolutely no way she was waiting another year or two!

It is possible - with a different personality that could tolerate the wait - that J might eventually have been truly 'ready' to learn to read without needing any particular help - like the Canadian youngsters mentioned - somewhere between the ages of twelve and fourteen.

If reading specialists were to enter unschooling homes, alternative schools and SDE facilities on a mission to 'identify' young dyslexics they would find plenty of them. The problem with diagnosis is that it is located within both time and context. Look a year or two later, and/or in a different context, and the 'problem' may be resolved. The other danger is that 'help' that isn't consensual can contribute to the problem.

If you take a listen to the interview with Justine McConville, one of the things that you will hear her observe is that "When there's an emotional wall around reading and writing - which you will see almost always if you're forcing it - that becomes the greatest barrier now. It's not phonetics or anything like that. It's that through the process of reading intervention this child has learned they are not able to, they're not smart enough, they can't do it, it's hard, it's not fun, it's stressful."

What if...

What if the optimal picture is to leave young people in charge of their own educational choices, while making sure that they are aware that there are accessible specialists on hand in case they choose to use them? And if they do use them, it's on their own terms.

There's no reason that J 'should have' had to wait till she was 14 and figure it out alone. Ms. S supported her in her own choice to read earlier, and at 11 she is getting active pleasure out of reading and writing right now, rather than having to wait. And, on the other hand, in a supportive SDE environment, it is possible that young people who

---

34   A hard philosophy and not for everyone, but possibly one reason why SVS graduates are famed for their ability to stop at nothing and just do what it takes to get into any college course they choose to, with no exam results or reports to show.

either don't want or don't manage to access a suitable assistant, will be just fine anyway, given time.

But let's concede, just for argument's sake, that there may be a subset of people who will never manage without professional help, and for whatever reason, don't feel the necessary motivation to get it. Maybe one in a thousand or one in ten thousand - some proportion small enough to have evaded both SVS and the other alternative schools reviewed here - alternative schools are always small, after all (one of the things that makes them so able to fulfil the core need for Relatedness).

What if some people with dyslexia really cannot manage to read without help, no chance whatsoever - but what if they also never get around to wanting help, and are 'allowed' to just go without it?

Ben Foss, another awesome DYSlexic who invented the text-to-speech Intel Reader, got so sick of being encouraged to work on his eye-reading that he actually asked his mother to imagine he was blind. Would she still try to get him to spend time learning to read - with his eyes - he asked her? There's eye-reading. There's also finger-reading (braille). And there's also ear-reading.

Ben is perfectly happy ear-reading, so, hey, what's the problem, Mom? Why pressure a person with DYSlexia to spend time on their eye-reading in this day and age? Ben had better things to do with his time, as do many young DYSlexics.

As Lynn points out in the conversation with Justine, the considerable time spent on reading remediation is time lost to the development of strengths, passions and talent. For young people it's also time spent not playing, at a point in history when we already know that play skills are crucial to success in life and learning. Reading remediation on top of an already heavy imposed curriculum can pretty much kill off discretionary time, robbing a young dyslexic both of opportunities to experience their own competence as well as opportunities to hone the gifts that could be their life's actual purpose.

The reasons for the disproportionate emphasis on eye-reading all have to do with the way school is currently (poorly) designed. Not because of our way of life today or in the future.

By offering early diagnosis and 'effective' intervention a certain number of 'dyslexics' can be 'helped' to 'fit in' and 'keep pace' with the standardised curriculum. For many this comes at a cost to self-esteem and a cost to the development of key talents. The argument is that it rescues their self-esteem from far worse damage and enables them to pass standardised tests.

However, let's notice that no damage whatsoever to self-esteem is inevitable in the first place, and standardised tests might not be the actual holy grail of a young dyslexic's life!

Take away the educational bias and social stress on literacy, and there's nothing to save them from.

I have come across exactly one story of a man who decided not to struggle at all, (because reading simply didn't interest him) and who did leave Britain's famous Summerhill school at 16, illiterate, by choice. I won't repeat the story of Freer here since I write about this in more detail in "Helping The Butterfly Hatch, Book 1: How Self-Directed Education Works and Why", but the condensed version is this: his self confidence was solid enough that he lived a very adventurous life travelling the planet for several years. Then when, as an adult he finally found a good reason to make the effort, he taught himself to read within two months, and eventually went on to get a degree in economics.

What Could Be Achieved By Liberating Dyslexics into Alternative Education?

I'm not going to say it. I will let someone with more expertise in DYSlexia say it:

"For decades dyslexic individuals have been expected to 'fit in', measured and benchmarked for the very skills they find challenging. Now, technology is replacing the need for these skills. In contrast dyslexic thinking skills are the 'in demand' skills in this changing world of work. Put simply the workforce of today and tomorrow needs dyslexic thinking, and dyslexic individuals should no longer be expected to 'fit in' but 'stand out', and focus on their strengths." — Kate Griggs, Made By Dyslexia

What I will say is: if by the time you finish reading this book you still think you can best achieve this by 'helping' Dyslexics 'fit in' to mainstream schooling systems, you probably also think that you can win a social media flame war if you just don't stop.

A Case Story and a Question

Case Story 1

Case Story 2 will describe a young person spontaneously resolving their reading 'stuck place' in a very sudden and spontaneous way.

This first story gives some insights into some of the ways young people might self-directedly work on their issues that are not as instant. It's hard for those of us who have no experience of Self-Directed Education to imagine how on earth young people can learn without being taught, or resolve difficulties without professional help. Observations of young people in classrooms don't help very much - once you train humans to behave in certain ways in certain circumstances, what you see will be the result of that training. Set them free, let them heal, and what you will see is very different. I have by now been blessed with the opportunity to directly observe a number of truly free young people. Let me tell you about one I am currently observing.

D is now ten years old. When she was three, her mother was convinced she'd be an early reader - maybe she'd even learn by the age of four. She was already interested in letters and words, and loved being read to. She was already putting in effort to memorise bits of one of her favorite stories so that she could 'read it' by turning the pages and saying the words.

However, as time went by, she somehow didn't progress beyond the idea that 'reading' meant remembering the story she'd received through her ears and reciting it back with the book as a prop. She didn't get the idea of linking a single 'word' to a single cluster of symbols on the page.

Her mother was an experienced SDE facilitator, and simply let things be. D had plenty of other interests and was clearly both bright and thriving. D's parents continued to read to her, and she was immersed in a house full of books, seeing her parents read all the time - so they knew it was inevitable that the time would come once she was ready.

An interesting interim stage took the form of communicating with friends and family on text using emojis to convey meaning rather than just as decoration, and writing lengthy wish-lists and to-do lists using pictures. (I have noticed this as a common stage in the learning-to-read process for SDE youngsters - starting with pictographic representation en route to using more abstract symbols.)

By the time D was eight, her mother strongly suspected she might have dyslexia - but there was still not really enough engagement with reading attempts for this to be clear. She sometimes complained about visual problems, particularly when engaging with text, but professional eye tests revealed nothing.

As she approached her ninth birthday, the interest in reading increased. She began to actively ask to 'do reading' together, and her parents obliged. One thing quickly became clear - the moment that anyone else got excited about her progress, expected her to want to read at a certain time because a routine was falling into place, invited her to read when she had not initiated it, encouraged her to keep going when she stopped, or tried to keep her 'on track' when her attention wandered... she would back off and not read again for weeks. And when everyone was careful not to do any of that, her reading work would still take place in fits and starts: refusing to put down the book until late at night for days in a row, and then gradually losing interest for a day or two, and then taking a complete break for a couple of weeks or months, and then flaring up with sudden desire once again. During this time she grasped the concept that letters map to sounds and letter combinations map to syllables and words, and she became able to chunk and sound out words. She managed a number of books on the level of 'Go Dogs Go!'

By now her mother was convinced she was dyslexic. 'House' became a sight word while 'the' and 'and' did not. In addition to the usual beginner habit of muddling 'b' with 'd' 'p', 'g' and 'q', fairly often 'I'm' would be read as 'my' and 'net' as 'ten', 'was' as 'saw', and even longer and more complex words would sometimes be scrambled. Sometimes a word carefully sounded out and triumphantly mastered would have to be sounded out completely from scratch again just a few words later, and then again a few lines down, and then again on the next page. C-h just wouldn't stick in her memory as 'ch' no matter how many times it was explained, and would be as likely to be interpreted as 'th' or 'sh'.

There was also a lot of pausing mid-sentence or even mid-word to notice something outside the window, or randomly remark on unrelated things that happened today, or criticise the illustrations or elements of story. Being SDE trained, her mother did not interpret this as a 'problem' but was able to respect it for what it actually was - a way to take a quick eye break, and reduce any feelings of anxiety and pressure. Being able to 'let her attention wander' was actually a helpful coping strategy that helped D be able to persevere.

As D approached her tenth birthday, behaviours that her mother considers 'self-remediation' began to appear. Until now all of her reading had been contextual - D would sound out all of the words, then repeat the sentence so that she could take in the story progression. Having mastered the basic oncept of reading as a way to access meaning, D now began to work on her 'problem areas' - decoding text with less context, and mastering the mechanics of spelling.

She began to pick random words to try, 'sharing the task' when her mother read to her. One favorite was doing the sound effects in Asterix comic panels - given that the illustrations offered no clues to distinguish between 'biff', 'bang', 'bong', or 'bonk', they were 'words' that could not be predicted but must be sounded out in their own right. She would also lie and cuddle as her mother read her own books, picking out short words scattered around the grown-up page. She stopped all other reading, and began writing. She started writing out 'project' pages on her favorite interests. She began texting her friends with words rather than emojis. She started writing a journal. She started writing down the songs she composed instead of just memorising them. Her mother knew better than to 'correct' her spelling - and her friends quickly learned that any helpful comments on her spelling would be met with a furious insistence that they mind their own business. She enjoyed spelling a word three different ways within two sentences, and defended this as her fundamental right. She was always willing to act as interpreter if people got stuck, as long as they were respectful of this right. One of the few things that was consistent was her use of 'tsh' in place of the English 'ch'. She did a lot of internet searches, and for these, she would ask people to tell her how to spell things 'correctly', and write down and copy the words she used often.

One fascinating day, she cheerfully approached her mother to share a triumph. She had proudly 'discovered' that 'ch' was more efficient than using 'tsh'.

Soon she began obsessively reading billboards and other signage, and number plates - text without much context that must be decoded more technically. She and her best friend then spent several days scrolling up their old text threads on Discord, laughing at their own spelling - a delight-filled process of mindful self-correction. Next, she started learning her favorite songs by ear, and then reading along with karaoke and lyric versions - which gave her exposure to a wide variety of fonts.

Then one night she spontaneously decided to try reading one whole Asterix speech bubble rather than just sound effects. To her delight she managed every word aside from 'campaign'. She then read the whole of the next two-page spread out loud to her mother, asking help with only a handful of words - most of them latin, and proper names such as 'Fulliautomatix'. She was triumphant, announcing "this just goes to show when I work on reading I can't do it, but when I take a break from reading, I learn all about it!" In her own mind the 'work' on billboards and karaoke songs was 'not reading' and 'just play'.

Noticing her own triumph and her own crowing about it, she then turned to her mother and sternly warned her to manage expectations "But just because I can read now, it doesn't mean I can write! They are not the same thing!" What a wonderful self-insight. A new intention took root.

She stayed up late that night consolidating her triumph by silently reading a full 15 pages of Asterix, asking for help with less than ten words, and proudly announcing that she hadn't had to ask for help with 'legionary'. She then fell happily asleep, proud of her completely owned achievement. "I just LOVE reading!" she said as she closed her eyes.

If you have had occasion to witness a tween girl in school receive instruction and remedial help for the same issues that D tackled...

Did you see anything like the empowerment, passion and delight in the process that D experiences? She has no concept of being 'behind' anyone. She is just loving her own literacy adventure.

In the world of school she would have been sent for diagnosis by age six, and everyone would have been worried. Very likely attempts to help would have triggered her resistance, and certainly have impacted her self-esteem. By nine, it's likely that even she herself would have been worried sick, and, given her personal neurology, under too much pressure to even look at a book. But, looking at this close up, seeing where she is now at ten, and how far she is likely to progress working at it like this for another eight stress-free years, we can see that by age eighteen indeed, her 'dyslexia' will likely be of the kind that Daniel Greenberg encounters. Most likely, invisible. A talent, a neurotype, a personal style, but not a 'case'.

Let's note that both D, as well as W who is featured in the story that comes later in this text, have known throughout that they could ask for help when needed. They might still ask for remedial support with reading or spelling - or anything else - in the years ahead. But it would be on their own terms, because they personally wanted it to happen, and it would be an expression of their empowerment, like asking for help with how to play the violin - not an expression of their inadequacy.

Why Is School Like It Is?

Back when schools first began, most young people got the bulk of their education outside of schools in non-text ways.

They learned through having long hours of unsupervised free play in nature with their peers, as well as by free-ranging around adult activities that they observed, assisted with, and were mentored in.

The 'reason' to go to school was to learn the few things that their parents couldn't help with in an era when few homes owned any book other than the Bible and many parents were illiterate themselves. School was for learning to read, write and calculate - the so-called '3R's'.

Those who were fluent readers could then further their education by going to those rare places where the few books available at the time were stored, such as monasteries and universities. Think of the terminology used to describe attending iconic institutions - one went off to 'read' mathematics at Oxford, or 'read' philosophy at Cambridge. These islands of academia were far removed from ordinary life, and 'learned men' could not easily access academic information in other ways unless they were wealthy enough to have a private library. (The private library being the only option for women!) Aside from the cost of books, only the rich had the leisure time for this kind of education, which became associated with high social and economic status.

Children of manual labourers often could not be spared even for basic schooling, so oral literacy had little social status and textual illiteracy became associated with low social and economic status.

In this way, we came to associate 'education' with being at the top of the status ladder and with reading and texts.

When the industrial revolution created the need for a mass of relatively unskilled labourers who were also able to read notices and instructions and fill in time cards and reports, school as we know it started to take form.

Since nothing very complex was required of these labourers, school was shaped like the factories it fed. The purpose of school was to ensure the ability to read and measure, to obey and meticulously follow apparently pointless instructions, and the ability to tolerate boredom and meaningless activity for the sake of external rewards. School also functioned to identify and sort the manual labourers from those with managerial potential. By forcing everyone to tackle a level of poorly presented academic material that most would find daunting, school also served to 'prove' to youngsters that those few who went on to tertiary studies and the associated wealth and status really 'deserved' to do so, preventing dissent.

Thanks to this history, schools are still modelled around the idea that children must be age-segregated in 'grades' and taught and tested on a predetermined sequential curriculum that is delivered in bite-size structured classes primarily through the medium of text.

In the 21st Century an increasing number of critics are pointing out that this is not an effective or efficient way to achieve real learning or the fulfilment of personal potential rather than just the ability to pass tests before forgetting the bulk of what has been studied.

However, cultural habits have momentum.

In order to cope with a content-heavy curriculum delivered largely through text, it is necessary to be able to read early and well, in order to not 'fall behind'.

(Take away this rather arbitrary demand, and there's no remaining correlation between early reading and success in either learning or life.)

Our continuing failure to shape our education services around real young people and their actual needs ensures that children who are not ready to read by the age of six at the latest, will struggle and suffer. They will not only 'fall behind', they will also lose confidence in themselves, something that can impact the rest of their lives.

Unfortunately there's a more sinister and recent reason for maintaining the toxic cultural habit of school as we know it. Keeping school as it is gives us a significant - now growing - number of children in distress, with parents desperate to support them.

Parents who haven't done their own research yet (many of us don't realise we need to, why should we have to?), generally believe the cultural myth that early eye-reading is key to education and life success. Parents love their kids. Parents who love their kids are a sucker market.

This means that there is a lot of money - more than $76 billion annually - to be made from specialised materials, tutoring and therapeutic services, with uncountable billions more for 'medications' for pediatric anxiety and depression.

Allowing profit motives to operate in the educational and wellness spheres guarantees the financial exploitation of children's misery.

Most service providers and educational innovators also believe the cultural myths - they aim to help, not contribute to the problem. However, they do have a strong incentive not to look too closely into what's actually going on.

"Educational systems... mainly protect the current status quo. That is a hard statement. And it may hurt a lot of good teachers. I know many in education work with hearts of gold. They give life, love and the best they can to our next generations. Yet, they also follow the ruling paradigms, sometimes fully convinced, sometimes crying and resisting, rebelling as best as they can. Often they feel or are caught in a web that has a craziness and life of its own." - Floris Koot.[35]

Enter the young person with dyslexia.

Instead of supporting the youngster in exploring the learning areas they are personally drawn to in the ways, with the people and at the times that work well for them, we insist that the goal must be to 'help' them 'fit in' with an imposed and standardised system. This turns out to be a profitable endeavour for those providing the 'help'.

Even beyond the financial benefits, there's also gains in terms of virtue-signalling and social status. 'Helping' 'learning-disabled' kids allows people to look good and to feel good about themselves. Either way there's little incentive for anyone to ask if all this is really in the 'best interests of the child'.

Cui Bono?

Not the young dyslexic.

---

35   Edushifts, edited by Greier and Gouvea https://www.edushifts.com/assets/ ebooks/EDUshiftsNow_Eng.pdf

Time For a New Normal?

Dr. Peter Gray who studies the role of freedom and play in learning, recently used an independent market research service to randomly survey families around children's anxiety levels under pandemic conditions. It turns out not only that school is more stressful than pandemic conditions, but that many children are absolutely thriving with more time at home, less pressure around learning, and more freedom to do their own thing.[36]

There's also a fascinating YouTube conversation between Kate Griggs from MadeByDyslexia and Rachel Berger from Microsoft[37] discussing recent experiences with remote learning. Griggs shares the results of an informal survey of the dyslexia community to find out how everyone is doing under pandemic conditions. It turns out that young people with DYSlexia are finding great benefit from many of the key conditions for Self-Directed Education - such as being able to do things at their own pace, manage their own activity/down-time flows, the opportunity to dig deep into what interests them, escaping from the writing down from blackboards and excessive reliance on text, being able to use tech at will, and - huge - escaping from the threat of exams for this year. Berger also mentioned the value of escaping from back-to-back classes in favour of a more fluid schedule, being able to take time for 'brain breaks' to process what's been taken in, and having more choice about when and how to learn, being more autonomous around meeting their own needs for movement, food and more. Maybe most important is the escape from environments that are stigmatising to those for whom eye-reading is not a natural strength, as well as a reduction in the quantity of prescribed course work.

Griggs makes the observation that pandemic learning conditions are probably a better fit with the work world that young people will eventually enter, than regular school conditions.

Let's take a moment to think about that. When the highly controlled,

---

36   https://www.psychologytoday.com/us/blog/freedom-learn/202004/is-the-pandemic-causing-children-s-anxi ety-go-or-down
37   https://youtu.be/tTFHOlwxRyQ

short back-to-back classes where you follow instructions, bells and obedience and standardisation model of school first came in, it was perfect preparation for factory work - which is what most people were fated for.

Factory workers - and people in fascist societies such as those for whom mainstream school was specifically invented - need high levels of obedience and actively suppressed levels of initiative, self-management, creativity and social responsibility. That's just not what we want to prepare youngsters for, today, is it? It's just not the future we face now.

The current cultural habit around education involves constant imposition, against and without consent, and without regard for the best interests of individual young people.

What we haven't sat down and realised collectively, is that this is actually for reasons of preparing young people to fit into factories and fascism.[38] Not for any reasons to do with actual education - optimal skills and knowledge for living a good life - as we think of it today.

"Modern conventional education is full of impositions on its students - such as what, how, and where students do, learn, behave, attend, participate, and communicate in the ways that the teacher and school define. For certain ages of students, schooling itself is compulsory in modern societies and, thus, imposed. However, the legitimacy of this imposition —how much of this imposition is necessary, useful, justified, and desirable for education itself —has not been specifically discussed and analyzed yet." - Eugene Matusov, University of Delaware[39]

There's a growing awareness that education needs to change, but seldom does anyone realise quite how far that change can safely - and ideally - go.

School as we know it has not succeeded in closing the poverty gap. It hasn't created an empowered populace. It has led us to a society where reliance on prescription and illegal drugs and other addictions are rife, and social, economic and political distress is the norm. It's led us to climate crises, social injustice, and more. School as we know it is as

---

38   It is ironic that so many countries claim to be trying to prevent resurgences of fascism by insisting on oppressively imposing schooling - guaranteeing a backfire!
39   https://files.eric.ed.gov/fulltext/EJ1148674.pdf

stacked against other marginalised groups as it is against those with DYSlexia - in fact the coercive and disempowering state of school as we know it renders all 'children' marginalised. They are the world's biggest marginalised group, and their suffering is simply fodder for jokes around how much kids hate school. That has been our normal for a long time now, so much that most of us just accept it as 'how things are'.

But, now that we are re-thinking so many things, and considering what we actually want a 'new normal' to look like...

What if ....?

What if what is good for those with dyslexia is actually good for all of us?

Coal miners in the UK used to take a canary down with them into the dangerous dark. Canaries are very sensitive to gas, and have delicate little lungs. If the canary passed out, the miners knew there was a gas leak, and had a chance to evacuate.

What if DYSlexics are the canaries of the school system?

What if, instead of giving them accommodations and tech-type gas masks... we should all get out?

"There are a lot of problems facing today's society... some of the most creative, innovative minds are at this moment atrophying behind bars. And that's all the result of a system that insists upon the most archaic form of educational medium - text," says Dean Bragonier as he proposes that we deliver compulsory curricula via tech instead.

How about distance learning as a better way to deliver a compulsory curriculum, even after the pandemic? say many others, now.

I love that so many people are realising that this is a key time to transform so many things in society, and create a 'new' normal rather than simply going back to the way things were previously done.

I love, absolutely love, that all these awesome people are coming up with all of these awesome ideas and resources and innovations. In the time that it will inevitably take to transform things more fundamentally, all of these trainings and outreaches and accommodations and modifications and supports and tech tools will make life a lot less miserable for as many young people as can be reached by them.

I also absolutely love what has been achieved by toy libraries, reading clubs and all of the other innovative explorations into informal education that have been successfully piloted in some of the least resourced communities of our world. And I am absolutely on fire with what I have personally observed, in SDE.

The danger in this moment, is that we lose an opportunity to realise how far we can actually go.

Like a young person with dyslexia who could really truly shine instead of merely being helped to 'keep pace' with non-dyslexic peers, our whole education system could undergo an enormous, wonderful and liberating transformation - instead of just implementing a few 'innovative' changes and otherwise carrying on in the mediocre and miserable way it did last year and the year before that.

As far as dyslexia is concerned, it's time to take a really good look at what's been achieved in alternative education.

It's criminal not to.

Instead of assuming that in the long-term it's enough to be supplying a standardised imposed curriculum through media other than text, or in places other than classrooms, or with assessments other than standardised tests, or with tech instead of text on paper... how about we stop and assess...

.... What if....

What if it might be better to stop using impositions such as curriculum altogether? What? Do without a curriculum?

What?!?

The Paradigm Shift Challenge: Where Do You Fit the Horse?

"The great obstacle to the development of the automobile was the lack of public interest. To advocate replacing the horse, which had served man through centuries, marked one as an imbecile." - Alexander Winton, reminiscing in 1930 on his founding of the Winton Motor Carriage company in 1897. (1930 was the year he retired, selling his successful company to General Motors.)

Imagine trying to explain to someone back in 1897, how a motor vehicle works, when what they think of as a 'car' is a horse-drawn buggy. Imagine showing them a drawing of a Benz. Imagine them asking 'where do you hitch the horse?' Imagine telling them that there's no horse involved. Imagine their astonishment. Their skepticism. Surely, there has to be a horse! And if there really, truly is no horse involved.... "You're crazy if you think this fool contraption you've been wasting your time on will ever displace the horse," Winton's banker chided him.[40]

Now let's consider education. For the last couple of hundred years education has increasingly been driven by imposed teaching and curriculum. All the 'innovations' currently being rolled out or developed have to do with teaching and curriculum. You improve the content or the layout or the pedagogical approach or the style of delivery or the accommodations. But you never, ever consider doing without imposed teaching and curriculum.

So, what have we done to 'help' those with dyslexia since realising that they are actually talented rather than doomed?

We've created Orton Gillingham which uses multisensory tactics to improve the effectiveness of delivering a phonics curriculum. We've created text-to-voice readers to deliver the content of various subject curricula via ear-reading. We advocate for accommodations to assist kids with dyslexia in having extra time or other concessions when it comes to writing tests and exams.

---

40   https://www.saturdayeveningpost.com/2017/01/get-horse-americas-skepticism-toward-first-automobiles/

But never, not ever, have we considered that maybe... What if....

... what if helping those with dyslexia 'cope better' with being taught and tested on an imposed curriculum is like making every motor vehicle lead a horse tethered behind it? What if all the remedial help and accommodations simply tether the horse tighter, and the very best of them put the horse on roller skates?

What we see when young people with dyslexia drop out of school or are liberated into SDE is, just how fast and far and smoothly they can actually go once they escape imposed teaching and curriculum!

What if the key difference between the 'juvenile delinquents' and the self-made millionaires is not a matter of whether or how much they got 'help' to 'fit in'. What if the difference is actually in whether they either lost faith in the value of their uniqueness, or managed to shrug everything off and maintain their own integrity until they could escape?

A car permanently leading a horse has to crawl along, stalling every now and then, or else damage the horse. Makes the car feel pretty ungainly, awkward, frustrated, shamed. Pointless. This is an analogy for: no matter how much you 'help' a young person with dyslexia 'keep pace' with non-dyslexic peers, all you're really doing is preventing the natural VROOOOOOOOOM of curious innovative exploration that is trying so hard to burst free.

What if they don't need to 'keep pace' with anything? What if all this 'help' is doing is just trying to bring the dyslexic to educational heel like an unruly dog? What if that involves breaking their spirit?

It's like taking a talented artist and insisting they do only paint-by-numbers kits. (And I have heard some schools even do that!)

Let's return to that conversation between Berger and Griggs. They both agree that there's been great benefit for young people with DYSlexia from relaxing so much of what's commonly considered central to education.

Let's think about that.

What prevents post-pandemic learning from allowing all of that too? And more?

School as we know it is all about keeping a large number of young people in one room at fixed times to complete fixed sections of work before they 'have to' go to the next class. That's what prevents dyslexics (along with all the other kids too) from generally having these helpful 'accommodations'. And if we think about it, all of these 'accommodations' are absolutely standard factors for optimising learning for all humans. So why is it so normal for us to sacrifice them?

We normally sacrifice these optimal conditions because the primary things we accommodate in our current education system are not people or their learning requirements.

The primary things we accommodate are the curriculum and the measures necessary to 'teach' it to an age-segregated group of kids all at the same time regardless of interest and readiness.

I have never met a kid with dyslexia (or any other kid for that matter) who had any great problem learning the things they were curious about. Dyslexic thinkers are exceptionally good at making a plan and overcoming any obstacles they encounter. I have never met one without an absolutely raging level of curiosity. I have never met one who 'needed' someone to tell them what to learn and how. I have never met one who needed teaching (as opposed to coaching, mentoring, stimulating interaction and human sounding-boards - they make plenty of use of those as and when they feel the need.) I have never met a dyslexic thinker who needed a curriculum.

It's pretty normal for dyslexics to resent teaching and curriculum. Just for fun, I invite you to try an internet search for famous people with dyslexia, and another for quotes about hating school, and take a look at the overlap. You might also want to look at this list here and the challenge the author suggests at the bottom.

https://www.psychologytoday.com/za/blog/freedom-learn/201107/what-einstein-twain-forty-eight-others-said-about-school

Last but not least, you could show your favorite dyslexic (if you didn't have one you wouldn't be reading this) the video 'Focus and Intensity' from Sudbury Valley School[41] and watch their response.

If my analogy fits, and making them stick with a taught curriculum

---

41   https://www.youtube.com/watch?v=NxPnvJE0V2E

is like making a car drag a horse along behind them so they can never go beyond second gear, then...

...Is there even one good reason to keep limiting dyslexic thinkers by tethering them to teaching and curriculum?

Dyslexics are natural auto-didacts.

No horse just means 0-60 in 1.9 seconds with a top speed of much, much more than a quarter horse. Full throttle. Great control on the bends.

Keeping Dyslexic Thinkers on Teaching and Curriculum For The Sake of Inclusivity, Instead of Socially Isolating them by Separating Them From Their Schooled Peers.

If this sounds like a good reason to keep young dyslexics 'in the system'... Let's consider firstly...

...that young people with DYSlexia are often studied, but seldom consulted.

In the one study I could find that actually respected their right to be heard on the issues that so intimately affect them, young people with DYSlexia preferred 'special schools' where they were actually valued and understood, rather than battling along in the mainstream where, even if they received 'help', they were stigmatised.[42]

However, like Jonathan Kozol[43], I have an innate horror of the idea of segregation of any kind, and a deep skepticism about how much good it does for those who are marginalised. So let's consider secondly, that maybe there's a way to liberate young people with DYSlexia from teaching and curriculum with no social isolation at all.

... how absolutely certain are we that non-dyslexic youngsters benefit from teaching and curriculum?

One excellent way to liberate young DYSlexics from their oppressive environments without segregating them, is to release them along with non-dyslexic peers into optimal non-coercive education.

---

42   Dyslexic learners' experiences with their peers and teachers in special and mainstream primary schools in North-West Province by Leseyane et al, African Journal of Disability ISSN: (Online) 2226-7220, (Print) 2223-9170
43   https://www.jonathankozol.com

It wasn't only the niche few who benefitted from the automobile, in the end… SDE has an excellent track record for non-dyslexics too…[44]

Horse-drawn buggies pretty much disappeared within a few decades.

Would you rather go down in history with motor-man Alexander Winton? Or with his banker?

---

44   (this book hasn't got space to go into that but take a look at my e-book Help! My Kid Hates School! as well as everything on website of the Alliance for Self-Directed Education at www.self-directed.org)

A Second Case Story and Some Fragments

Case Story 2

W's mother's curiosity was piqued the first time he drew a realistic humanoid figure. He was about four years old. He drew the figure in landscape, as if lying down, but posed as if standing. Then he turned the paper to portrait position and stuck it on the wall. When asked, he confirmed that he had intended the figure to be standing. She asked why he had drawn it sideways instead of just drawing it the other way in the first place. He just shrugged.

When W was five years old he knew a few letters of the alphabet, and his mother was (gently) trying to teach him more. This was tricky, because he became extremely annoyed about the fact that different fonts could be used for the same letters.

On top of this, W was extremely strong-willed. "If you want him to NOT do something, suggest it!" his mother would often sigh.

One day when she had just managed to finally get him to sit down with a pencil and actually copy a few letters - hallelujah! - he tossed his pencil aside, leapt up, and tipped out his basket of toy weapons. Taking a deep breath, because she was a non-coercive mother, she watched him write his name using plastic swords and pistols. At the time she found this frustrating. Later when she had learned about both Orton Gillingham and SDE, she realised this was yet another example of the wisdom inherent in the self-educating drives.

The interest didn't last. Nor did it completely fade. Every few months he would become interested in reading and writing - for a few days. Then, the interest would disappear again, eclipsed by activities such as playing with magnets, climbing trees, learning to cycle, and throwing dust and other items into the wind over and over again, to see what would happen. With hindsight, she remembers that there was also a lot of interest in finding Wally in the 'Where's Wally' series - something that trains the eye to distinguish figure from ground and focus on detail while dealing with a lot of 2D visual complexity.

65

Because she was by now studying Self-Directed Education, his mother tried not to worry when he still wasn't reading by age six. Nor by age seven. Nor did she allow herself to worry when he was only able to manage basic three-letter words, (and only on 'good days', and only words such as 'cat' and 'dog' not words such as 'the' and 'and') by age 8. The average age for 'naturally' learning to read is 8.5, she had now learned, with a wide spectrum on either side.

Since he loved to criticise toy 'aeroplanes' in terms of whether they would actually fly in real life, based on the aerodynamics implied by their design, he was clearly bright enough. And given he could even explain to a post-grad physics student at a university recruitment exhibition exactly why and how their magnetic levitating 'flying pan' must have been constructed, he was obviously learning something with all of his self-directed activity - measuring how high his home-made catapults could toss things and dreaming up fantastic alternative energy ideas - even if not reading yet. (She remarked to friends on his advanced understanding of magnets before being able to read the word 'magnet'.).

Then came the day, close to his 9th birthday, when he wrote his name backwards on a piece of paper and walked around for a full half hour saying loudly 'is this forwards or backwards? I can't make up my mind!' With a sigh, his mom admitted to herself that this was actually just the final 'message' she needed to convince her that it was time she looked into dyslexia.

The first few resources she found were horrid. They made dyslexia sound a lot like leprosy. Then, she discovered 'The Gift of Dyslexia' by Ron Davis. Aha! Dyslexia is actually a talent? Yup, that sounded like her boy, at last. Ron Davis had a method to help dyslexics read, and sure enough, there was a licensed therapist in their town. Now to raise the funds for sessions. But, being a committed SDE mom by now, she discussed this with her son, before booking a session. She told him the good news - that it seems that maybe he has the same kind of brain as Leonardo Da Vinci (a recent interest of his.) She then described to him what she had read in the book, about how dyslexia worked with regards to reading. He translated this into his own words: "You're telling me I need to change gears when I read?"

That night he started reading full sentences (reading was always pushed over to late at night, once the wonderful outdoors became inaccessible). After a while fatigue set in and he scrambled a word. "I think you've slipped gears" she said, and he corrected the word and carried on.

In the following month he finished several MagicTreehouse books before finding the series annoying. Slime Squad came next, followed by Nancy Drew.

He spent a significant period (several weeks, maybe even a couple of months, his mother isn't sure in hindsight) 'having to' read out loud while he gradually trained himself to read silently, passing through stages of whispering and sub-vocalising, on the way. Fortunately he was not in any situations where peers would tease him for this, so he was simply free to do what he needed to do. And it seems that what he needed to do was use his eyes to help him ear-read to himself, until eye-reading and ear-reading became integrated.

Within 18 months he had chomped his way through the whole of the Harry Potter series, and all things Percy Jackson. He exhausted Eoin Colfer. The Eragon books went down easy. He also devoured all of the stand-alone junior material his mom could find, and then, given his tender age combined with his now advanced reading level, his mom turned to Terry Pratchett, handing him one after the next including all the 'grownup' books, which he ploughed through - twice.

And... he still couldn't spell the word 'people' without going to a keyboard to help him figure it out.

But hey who cares about that when you're busy simulating everything Space-X does, in Kerbal Space Program...

At the age of 15 he's not currently reading much fiction. However, he greatly enjoys interactively reading parts ranging from King Duncan to Lady MacBeth, out loud and on the fly, in a group that meets weekly for a couple of hours of Shakespeare. Aside from that, he's too busy calculating the gravity dynamics of hypothetical roller-coasters, tackling boolean logic in order to build a 'nand-to-tetris' project as a fun way to hang out with a couple of his friends 'and fill out my math/s gaps' (he's still not ever sat down to do a page of long-division but that's a topic for another e-book!), earning pocket money by subcontracting for his first 3D digital modelling piece-job, studying web-design with the aim of doing the same, and exploring elements of game design. None of which he could spend much time on if he was busy working on his spelling and handwriting, passing Geography and English grammar and making sure his uniform was neat and his hair was short (it's not).

Let's note that he's never had a formal lesson in anything but parkour and trumpet-playing (and a couple of drama lessons that he found annoying). Instead, he searches for what he needs online, experiments with things in the yard, the kitchen and the fireplace, and seeks out real life conversation with knowledgeable and interesting people. As a result his social skills and research skills are really, really solid.

However, at 15 he still can't spell the word 'people' without going to a keyboard to help him figure it out. But he doesn't see any problem with this. He's managed to make progress composing a couple of sci-fi short stories and never has any problem writing what he needs for searching the web for the tutorials he prefers to use instead of structured courses. And whenever (occasionally) someone suggests that he do things to a piece of actual paper with a sharp instrument, he reacts as if this is very obviously a case of disrespect for his basic human rights. He makes the most wonderful digital birthday cards for the family. He can't wait for neurolink to be accessible.

When discussing the creation of this text with him, and conversing around the idea of remedial education, he said simply "I have always needed to learn stuff in a different way."

His 'mental picture' of remedial help is of adults trying to force a child to walk into a wall, again and again and again and again... when left to their own initiative they could simply walk around it.

Would it have been better to send him to school at 5 and give him lots of Orton Gillingham and other remedial support to get him reading a few years earlier (at the cost of most of his self-directed physics explorations) and put in the hard work to save his self-esteem?

What do you honestly think: would it have been in this dyslexic's best interest to rather send him to school and 'help' him 'keep pace' with his peers?

If you do think so, I would like to hear your arguments.

A Couple Of Snippets

- An SDE facilitator's 8 year old niece came to stay with her aunt for a few days during the holidays. The (BIPOC, working class) family were very stressed that this child 'could not read' and was doing terribly at school. The aunt, who had a great relationship with the child already, simply made sure there were plenty of simple books she knew her niece would love - due to their themes and content and pictures - just lying around. Sure enough, her niece picked them up to look at, and soon exclaimed excitedly to her aunt 'Look! I can read this, and they say I'm no good at reading, but I can read this!"

- Identical twins in SDE were learning to read and write, mostly through creating their own little 'books' and reading them back to themselves and their friends. One wouldn't write down a single word without being sure it was spelled 'correctly'. The other rejoiced in her own creative spelling and treated it as an exciting form of research to check whether the SDE facilitator could understand what she'd written. Both were loving every minute of their journey, because it was theirs.

- In response to an alternative education email forum thread that elicited several responses to my call for input for this text, I received this: "I think you are right that the main issue is when the student wants to learn and when the student is ready to learn. Among other things, I believe that a lot of cases of dyslexia come from forcing students to learn too soon. When they are ready they will somehow learn." - this from Jerry Mintz, founder of the Alternative Education Resource Organisation. Let's note that beyond being a public educator for many years before becoming principal of an alternative school, he has also run multiple interactive education conferences over many years, as well as helped found numerous alternative schools in America and abroad. In other words, he's seen 'em all!

If you enjoyed these case stories and snippets and want to explore more on how young people learn to read in SDE, there are some suggestions for you in the 'further exploration' section.

The key thing to realise is that learning to read can take a huge range of forms and very often SDE facilitators and unschooling parents don't actually know how individual young people have learned to read - only that they have managed it.

If we look at the case stories of W and D, they do not learn other educational material by being allowed to ear-read and submit their classwork digitally, but by - inter alia - learning 'out of sequence', using YouTube tutorials and access to people who can answer direct questions.

They learn to write and read by being free to use creative spelling for active communication without being shamed; by learning by memorising favorite song lyrics then reading along with the karaoke instead of having to toil through 'See Jane sit.' In other words - by doing what fits them individually. But.

Force all the kids in the class to do karaoke or surf YouTube and you will quickly find that there's a whole new group of 'learning differences' since nothing whatsoever suits everyone. There are cars with electric engines, cars with combustion engines - some of which run on gas while others use diesel or biofuels, cars in all different shapes, automatic, manual, with engines of all different sizes. The bottom line is, the difference between a car and a carriage is - the car has no horse!

What if the difference between education that's optimal for dyslexics - and all of us - and education that handicaps some - or all - of us is: that each person can learn what, when and how it suits them best, with no external impositions?

None. No imposed curriculum. No imposed methods. No imposed timing. No imposed physical environments. No imposed companions/ mentors/teachers. No imposed tests/evaluations/grading. No imposed goals/outcomes.

No. External. Impositions.

Dyslexics thrive when they self-direct. What if ...

What if anything less is actually disabling? That's what I propose. What do you say?

What If You Don't Agree With Anything This Book Says?

So by this point I'm guessing we probably have three kinds of feelings happening for readers of this text. Maybe more, but here's the three I'm guessing are prominent.

Some of you may be feeling something like 'Wow! I'm going to see what I can do to make it possible for my favorite dyslexics to liberate themselves from the school thing".

Others may be feeling something like "This is all very thought provoking but I'm going to have to chew on it all before I decide where I stand".

And some of you are likely feeling something like "What rubbish! You can't convince me of any of this!"

We live in an era where it's impossible to 'prove' anything, and where 'evidence' is available to cherry-pick according to what you prefer to prove. Go looking now and you will find everything from 'proof' that Orton Gillingham works, to 'proof' that it makes zero difference. You will find at least one academic study concluding that dyslexia is a myth. You will find people busting the 'myth' that dyslexia involves any advantage or talent. You will find people insisting that early diagnosis is the only hope. You will find people insisting that non-interference and completely consent-based support prevents there ever being a problem. Pick your stance and you will be able to back it up.[45]

So just for argument's sake, let's say I'm wrong about everything else, here's the one way school absolutely, incontrovertibly creates DYSlexia.

---

45   The current unpopularity of Truth and Goodness is also a direct creation of school, but again, beyond the scope of this booklet to explore. See my Patreon post here for some thought-starters https://www.patreon.com/posts/31788878

One Way That School Absolutely, Incontrovertibly Creates DYSlexia:

What proportion of the population has Dysculinaria? How many have Dysautomobilia?

Dysequinaria?

No idea? Why not?

Some people really cannot cook, no matter how hard they try. I've personally met at least two. No, really, it's a thing.[46] I can think of a few execrable drivers who really don't seem negligent, just very... not talented, as well as a few who completely 'refuse' to learn to drive at all. The ability to cook, and the ability to drive a car, are both fundamental skills necessary for responsible adult life in our culture. So why don't we care if young people 'graduate' from school without being able to do either?

Riding a horse? Not so much in this day and age, but try being a society success without a 'good seat' a few generations back.

Well, yes, you can pay or persuade other people to cook for you, and to drive for you, and horse-sense in the 21st Century is completely optional.

Same with reading! One of Sir Richard Branson's keys to success is that he hires people to do the things he's not so good at. In the 21st Century, you don't even need to be able to afford a personal assistant. Even if state-of-the-art text-to-voice is not an option, you can get a workable option online for free.

As Justine McConville says (in that conversation I'm reminding you to listen to as soon as you finish reading this), "it's normal for people to have brains that are better at some things and not as good at other things - that's true of every single human being."

Why single out the brains that don't excel at eye-reading?

---

46   https://www.researchgate.net/publication/278025995_Cooking_Disability

If schools insisted that every child successfully prepare a cooked breakfast according to a new recipe every day before they could study anything else, Dysculinaria would be a learning disorder of note. Likewise if all teens had to drive themselves to school, or if there were no access to school grounds without riding there on horseback every day.

In this day and age, it is no longer necessary for an optimal education to depend on - be held hostage by - one's level of ability to eye-read.

It's important to note that young people from socially or economically disadvantaged families who are already struggling with systemic racism or other forms of prejudice and oppression that impact their self-perception, could be even more vulnerable to the additional pressures around reading competence.[47]

The well-meaning efforts to 'leave no child behind' can really backfire horribly, especially for children from under-resourced homes who actually need more time to play and more opportunities to experience their own empowerment. It's interesting that small SDE facilities closely resemble a 'rich home environment' and therefore may in and of themselves offer a kind of natural remediation, giving disadvantaged youngsters a chance to catch up later on what they didn't get in their early years. On the other hand classrooms that pressure young children into focussing on literacy can end up depriving them of opportunities to develop other important skills.

Because what we DO need on those occasions where we really need to eye-read and can't, and we have no money, and we can't even access any voice-to-text options, is someone to do it for us for free. And that's a matter of two other skills: social skills, and self-confidence.

To the extent that our childhood circumstances and education have allowed us to emerge with good social skills and with self-confidence intact, we will still be okay. Schooling experiences that have undermined these two skills - such as having a hard time year after year in remedial classes - could be the nail in the coffin.

Let's recall Roger Clarke's study of Successful Illiterate Men.

---

47   Interdisciplinary Journal of Teaching and Learning Volume 3, Number 3Fall 2013 159 Educating Black Males With DyslexiaShawn Anthony RobinsonDoctoral CandidateCardinal Stritch University https://files.eric.ed.gov/fulltext/EJ1063059.pdf

What he found was key to understanding the impact of the artificially high status of reading in our society that the cultural myths propagated by school have created.

The 'disabling' factor in their lives was not their illiteracy, but had to do entirely with the social stigma of being illiterate. This stigma was strong enough that it even interfered with their motivation to further their education and upgrade their reading abilities. (Spot the vicious cycle?)

Why is there a stigma about illiteracy? Because school has created a cultural expectation that everyone should be able to read. And a belief that if you can't read, that's shameful. Further, school makes efficient eye-reading into a key that unlocks the rest of education. Fail to master that one key, and you fail the rest. By artificially elevating the importance of eye-reading, school has turned even any slight 'weakness' in reading into a full-fledged disability. Presumably in order to try to create 'motivation' in people who are stressed out and don't want to be there, school also promotes the terrifying myth that lack of success at school equals lack of success as an adult.

On those occasions in SDE where a young person does become stressed and/or ashamed about not being able to read yet, it's generally due to negative messages from non-SDE people and media around them, propagating these myths. It's possible that even beyond impacts on self-esteem for SDE kids, it might even sometimes have enough impact on morale to delay their reading acquisition. However, it seems convincing to me that, as long as they remain in optimal SDE circumstances, they will nevertheless be more okay than if they went into mainstream school.

Even better, giving young people the right and ability to choose non-coercive education options, within a context of the positive societal reframing around dyslexia that MadeByDyslexia is working to achieve, could give us an enormously different picture when it comes to the difference in incidence between Dyslexia - the advantageous neurology, and DYSlexia, the learning disability.

Let's consider a few quotes pulled together into a paper entitled "Dyslexia and inclusion: Time for a social model of disability perspective?" by Barbara Riddick.[48]

Referring to the findings of Oliver and Barnes she points out that "although individuals may have impairments these are only transformed into disabilities by the negative attitudes of the society they live in. From this perspective the impairments underlying dyslexia have only become a major difficulty because of the move towards mass literacy and the consequent negative connotations attached to being 'illiterate'. Because mass literacy was attendant on mass schooling the notions of being 'educated' and being 'literate' have become inextricably bound together in many European cultures."

She goes on to say that "The underlying tenet of inclusion is that the school should adapt its practice to accommodate the child....in the spirit of inclusion this would suggest that as well as an intervention model focused on 'improving' children's performance we need to consider whether a social model which challenges some of our beliefs and assumptions about literacy is needed."

In other words, what if we need to stop telling everyone that school is necessary for education, and that reading is necessary for education? The current myth suggests that this will be a disaster - everyone will stop bothering to learn, and stop bothering to read.

The reality experienced in SDE suggests that the opposite might be possible. Set free from artificial pressure, reading might be more likely to become a universal skill, and education more likely to come alive, and become life-long.

The bottom line is actually not about reading, but about the way young people are treated. It's time to consider giving them human status - also a topic that's beyond the scope of this text, but that I invite you to explore, using the 'further exploration' section as a way to start.

Bottom line - humans are human no matter the age. It's a huge mistake to treat young people 'like children' in the sense of automatically imposing on them without their consent and against their well-being, just for adult comfort and convenience. I am willing to bet you that's why there's so much DYSlexia in schooling systems

48   Barbara Riddick (2001) Dyslexia and inclusion: Time for a social model of disability perspective?, International Studies in Sociology of Education, 11:3, 223-236, DOI:10.1080/09620210100200078

that paternalistically impose on young people, and little or maybe even none in education approaches that don't.

Dyslexic thinkers are unusually creative and capable people. What if ....

What if they can most often figure out how to learn to read ....

... even better than we can figure out how to reliably help them learn? What if....

What if we.... Set them free?

Or, better yet, set them FHREE?[49]

I might be completely wrong about all of my speculations and hypotheses here. Or others might be mistaken about things they currently deeply believe to be true.This book is not intended to be a last word on anything. What it is, is an invitation to explore some rather wonderful possibilities.

I said it before and I will say it again.

> **Nobody can yet say for absolute sure what is or is not True about Dyslexia vs DYSlexia. But nobody can say that it's not worth the bother to find out.**

---

49   http://www.fhree.org/

Further Exploration list

There are a number of resources in the footnotes of this text, they are not repeated here. This is a list of additional resources you might like to explore. It's the proverbial ice-berg tip.

Non-Coercion in Education:

www.educationconsent.me

www.fhree.org

www.youthrights.org/issues/student-rights/

Dyscalculia:

John Lockhart - A Mathematician's Lament

Transforming public school:

Derry Hannam - Another Way Is Possible

Jerry Mintz - School's Over: How to Have Freedom and Democracy in Education

Wayne Jennings - School Transformation

Self-Directed Education:

Daniel Greenberg - Free At Last

Greenberg et al - The Sudbury Valley School Experience

Peter Gray - Free To Learn book, and also YouTube talk https://youtu.be/qT18r_74kyw

Je'anna Clements - Helping The Butterfly Hatch, Book 1: How Self-Directed Education Works and Why, and Book 2: How Can We Support Young People In Self-Directed Education?

www.self-directed.org

www.sudburyvalley.org

Dyslexia:

Ron Davis - The Gift of Dyslexia

Short animation 'Float' - by Pixar on Disney: My interpretation of this is that Dyslexia can fly - and curriculum, a structured school day, testing, evaluation, and the artificial loading put on eye-reading, are the rocks in the backpack.

Learning to read in home education:

Harriet Pattison - Rethinking Learning to Read
https://etheses.bham.ac.uk/id/eprint/5051/

Alan Thomas - Informal Home Education: Philosophical Aspirations put into Practice
https://link.springer.com/article/10.1007/s11217-012-9299-2?shared-article-renderer

Renuka Ramroop - Natural Learning in the South African Context: a Critical Analysis
http://ulspace.ul.ac.za/bitstream/handle/10386/3001/ramroop_sr_2019.pdf?sequence=1&isAllow ed=y

www.home-education.org.uk/articles/article-research-review.pdf

FHREE

FULL HUMAN RIGHTS-
EXPERIENCE EDUCATION

www.fhree.org

Printed in Great Britain
by Amazon